MALE vs. MAN

MALE vs. MAN

HOW TO HONOR WOMEN, TEACH CHILDREN, AND ELEVATE MEN TO CHANGE THE WORLD

DONDRÉ WHITFIELD

ZONDERVAN BOOKS

ZONDERVAN BOOKS

Male vs. Man
Copyright © 2020 by Dondré Whitfield

Requests for information should be addressed to:
Zondervan, *3900 Sparks Dr. SE, Grand Rapids, Michigan 49546*

Zondervan titles may be purchased in bulk for educational, business, fundraising, or sales promotional use. For information, please email SpecialMarkets@Zondervan.com.

ISBN 978-0-310-36617-1 (softcover)
ISBN 978-0-310-35715-5 (audio)

Library of Congress Cataloging-in-Publication Data

Names: Whitfield, Dondré T., 1969- author.
Title: Male vs. man : how to honor women, teach children, and elevate men to change the world / Dondré Whitfield.
Other titles: Male versus man
Description: Grand Rapids : Zondervan, 2020. | Includes bibliographical references. | Summary: "In Male vs. Man, actor, social activist, and restoration coach Dondré Whitfield offers males a heart-to-heart look at what it takes to become a true man—one that lives righteously—and informs men how to find joy and purpose in serving their families and communities"— Provided by publisher.
Identifiers: LCCN 2019049789 (print) | LCCN 2019049790 (ebook) | ISBN 9780310357131 (hardcover) | ISBN 9780310357148 (ebook)
Subjects: LCSH: Men—Conduct of life. | Men—Identity. | Men—Religious life.
Classification: LCC BJ1601 .W45 2020 (print) | LCC BJ1601 (ebook) | DDC 248.8/42—dc23
LC record available at https://lccn.loc.gov/2019049789
LC ebook record available at https://lccn.loc.gov/2019049790

Author is represented by Leticia Gomez, Savvy Literary Services, www.savvyliterary.com.

Cover design: Curt Diepenhorst
Cover photo: Rowan Daly
Interior design: Kait Lamphere

Printed in the United States of America

22 23 24 25 26 27 28 29 30 31 32 33 /LSC/ 16 15 14 13 12 11 10 9 8 7 6 5 4 3 2 1

To my son, Dré—
to you and your daily matriculation into manhood.
To my daughter, Parker—
with the prayer that you will forever be covered
by my book's definition of a Man.
To my wife, Salli—
for being a part of my manhood's master class.
I hope that I have become
the Man of your dreams and desires.
And finally, to my mom—
while you couldn't teach me to be a Man,
you taught me all the essential things
that have shaped who I have become.

CONTENTS

PREREQUISITE

Helping males grow into *Men* is vitally important to me.* What I will share in this book is born out of a lifetime of experiences, many of them filled with failure and several seasons of empathetic healing. My life was forever changed the day I realized the following: every man you meet is a male, but not every male you meet is a *Man*. That realization has changed the trajectory of my life.

I had a tough time matriculating into my manhood. I didn't have my biological father to provide proper guidance, but other males provided the messaging of what is now considered toxic masculinity culture. Despite having a mother who taught me to the contrary, the streets (in my case, the Bushwick neighborhood of Brooklyn), pop culture's messages, and the spoils of accomplishment attracted me. I wanted to be the kind of guy who had power from accomplishments, money, and notoriety—to have

---

* Throughout the book, I'm capitalizing and italicizing each use of the word *man* when it describes a mature *Man*, particularly when it is used in comparison to the term *male* or *grown male*, which is always lowercased.

a reputation of being a "guy's guy" and a "ladies' man." I wanted to fight when someone disrespected me, and to be of service to myself.

Once I grew spiritually and matured past that way of thinking, I wanted to give other guys the information that helped me in my transformation. That's when I was urged to write this book—even though I didn't want the burden due to all my other responsibilities. But when I thought about my journey, and especially the *pain* it produced, I knew the journey had a *purpose*, and I knew I had to honor it.

Fifteen years ago, my best friend, Amon Parker, wanted to learn to ride a motorcycle. I was an experienced rider who would often do wheelies—front wheel in the air while balancing on the back wheel—down the street. The front wheel would be so high in the air that it would be in the "11:30" position. I couldn't see over the speedometer, but I'd peek around the body of the bike to see where I was going. I would also do stoppies—stopping suddenly to send the back wheel in the air while balancing the motorcycle on its front wheel. I was courageous and reckless, and I spent countless hours perfecting these maneuvers.

Ironically, I told Amon he had to take a motorcycle safety course before we could ride together. He agreed to do so. We got him a loaner from a manufacturer, and he was ready to ride! I picked him up from his home for his first day of riding on the freeway. I told him I would "look out and look after him." We said goodbye to his wife, daughter, and son, and off we went.

Life was perfect! It was a beautiful day. We visited all the major biker stops. Amon was in his glory. Onlookers admired our speed machines, decked out in custom colors and chrome. His only disappointment that day was that he was on a "stock" machine and not his own. He went on and on about his plans to customize a bike once he bought one.

His spirit was unlike anyone I've ever been friends with. We were eerily similar in the way we approached life—*energetically*. Those close to him called him the "hyped man." He could turn the most mundane activity into something interesting and exciting.

In motorcycling, that kind of energy can work against you— particularly at high speeds. I know because it had worked against me a few times. But the day was going perfectly. We didn't have a care in the world. After one of our stops, we remounted and hit the freeway. For his first time on the freeway, he was doing great.

We were joined by another biking friend of mine. He and I did wheelies, stoppies, and other tricks simultaneously as Amon watched in awe and envy. I told him, "Soon, brother! One step at a time." He nodded in reluctant agreement. I could tell it was driving him crazy.

We came to a section of the freeway that had a big sweeping turn. My experienced friend and I could navigate this turn without even thinking. We had done it a million times. Knees down in the turn, doing about 70–80 miles per hour. Blazing fast. Not a care in the world. Before we went into the turn, I communicated to Amon with hand signals that it was coming up and that my friend and I would go up ahead, but that he needed to slow down. He nodded reluctantly, and I proceeded into the turn at full speed. It would be the last time I saw my best friend alive.

We don't know if a car hit him or if he lost control as he went into the turn too fast, trying to follow my lead, but Amon was gone. I didn't fulfill my promise to "look out and look after" him—my friend, my brother—and it was irreversibly devastating. While I had lost a friend, a wife lost a husband, two kids lost a father, a mother lost a son, a sister lost a brother, and the world lost a great *Man*! It changed our lives forever.

I felt so much guilt and responsibility. My daughter, my first child, who was born a few months later was named after him—Parker. The profound pain produced by his loss activated me to pursue manhood with greater vigor.

After his loss, I hurt like I can't describe, the kind of pain that is debilitating. I finally found relief from studying the Bible with *Men* who understood my struggle and trauma. They offered me great counsel through its word that helped with every facet of my walk as a *Man*. Now before you close this book because you don't have a relationship with God or you call God something different, have a different faith, or have no faith at all, let me simply say that this book—while I use biblical references to explain how I have processed certain things—has *nothing* to do with religion. The messaging about manhood here is not about how you feel about God; it's about the universal value and this messaging that is for everyone. I write through the lens of how I received it. Please don't discard this message because you dislike some of its sourcing.

Many people love ketchup. Some can't stand the taste or consistency of a tomato, so they don't eat tomatoes. (I used to be one of those people.) But while they dislike tomatoes, they don't discard ketchup. They dislike the source but don't discard what it produces, because it brings them value. I've learned life lessons from people and things that don't completely line up with my belief system. But I don't rebuke the lessons simply because they don't speak to who I am or what I believe. I can still receive the nutrients that come from them. That's what we must do to elevate ourselves. If we rely on everything to be in total alignment with our beliefs or feelings for something to be perfect, we'll be at a total deficit our entire lives. *Men* have enough awareness to know they need to seek out the value in something and invest it for their ongoing growth. Know this: I'm not selling church or God in this book; I'm selling manhood and its value to our women, children, and community.

As I've stated, the experiences that led me to my own manhood were not without pain, but thankfully they were also not without purpose. In fact, my pain was exactly what served to inform my purpose. (More on that later.) I would not be able or even qualified to pen these pages without the blows that life has dealt to me and that have edified me. Extracting the lessons from life's obstacles and diligently applying them have made me a success. Notice that I haven't mentioned anything about my vocation playing into that equation. I have learned that being accomplished and being successful are two entirely different things.

I know many entertainers, CEOs, athletes, and other standouts who are incredibly accomplished males. Their résumés, houses, cars, bank accounts, jewelry—the accoutrements of "success" by society's standards—all prove that they know how to use their gifts, talents, and knowledge for monetary gain. However, the trail of broken relationships they leave in their wake makes me unable to call them truly successful. And it reveals that they're not mature *Men*.

I believe that a *Man* who is truly successful is one with healthy and whole relationships. Thus, the women in a successful *Man*'s life usually feel honored, covered, protected, and heard. My goal every day is to make my mom, my wife, my daughter, and all the other sisters in my path (related or not) feel that way as well.

We need to make sure the differences between males and *Men* are clear. It is a sad commentary when there is no clear distinction between former president Barack Obama and a sexual predator, or between Bishop T. D. Jakes and a rapist, Joel Osteen and a murderer, or you and me! In the minds of society, we are all technically and biologically just males whom everyone unconsciously calls "men." The truth of the matter is that we are *not* all *Men*. That's what this book is all about.

Men are accountable. *Men* willingly take responsibility. *Men* lead their lives and homes in a servant leadership manner every day! Are they perfect? No! However, they are intentional about living righteous lives and holding themselves to a higher standard than the average male who is addicted to living according to the appetites of his flesh rather than resisting this urge for the sake of pursuing a godly life.

I'll be referring to "the flesh" and "the Spirit" in this book. These words come from the Bible, but I emphasize again that you don't need to be a believer to receive the information presented in this book. I apply biblical references practically and use them to plainly lay out a map to manhood.

In the gospel of John, Jesus used these phrases in this way: "The Spirit gives life; the flesh counts for nothing. The words I have spoken to you—they are full of the Spirit and life."[1] Later in the Bible, the apostle Paul used these words again: "Those who live according to the flesh have their minds set on what the flesh desires; but those who live in accordance with the Spirit have their minds set on what the Spirit desires. The mind governed by the flesh is death, but the mind governed by the Spirit is life and peace."[2]

In simpler terms, the flesh points to the thing inside us that wants to serve ourselves, while the Spirit is that which lives in us that looks to be of service to others. You will begin to see how grown males generally navigate life by succumbing to the flesh, while *Men* navigate life by submitting to the Spirit. Living by "the flesh" versus by "the Spirit" will help us see the differences between a *Man* and someone who is merely a male.

Now to be completely transparent, I have not always operated in a state of manhood myself. I struggle like all males, but like all *Men*, I seek to elevate my manhood daily. The key is simply being honest with oneself. We all have both strengths and weaknesses. For me, I know that when it comes to living by the flesh, I am a recovering addict, and I govern myself accordingly.

I wake up every day choosing to be "Discipled Dondré" rather than "Brooklyn Dré." Brooklyn Dré is the fleshly version of myself who's looking for a fight, looking to be physically satisfied, and craving to have his ego well-fed. That dude, left to his own devices, will wreck my life because of his selfish agenda. With that said, both Brooklyn Dré and Discipled Dondré are quite knowledgeable when it comes to life's "fires." The difference between the male and the *Man* battling within me every day is that one is a firefighter who puts out fires, while the other is a straight arsonist. It is crucial that we thoughtfully acknowledge our battle of male and *Man* so we are reminded that we must *choose* to be a firefighter.

Firefighters understand the importance of fireproofing. A good firefighter—a *Man*—can recognize fire hazards and therefore work diligently to *prevent* them. Remember Smokey Bear? In one of the longest-running public service campaigns, the ad stated, "Only you can prevent forest fires." (It was actually changed to "wildfires" in 2001.) But I trust you get the point.

However, a "grown male" who functions in the capacity of a

resident arsonist is an entirely different story. A grown male's presence is a constant and consistent stream of chaos, but in varying degrees. As a matter of fact, he is a person who starts fires just for the sake of starting fires. I suspect you know a male like this. We all do. He's the type of guy who starts arguments, is irresponsible, and refuses to take accountability for anything. Additionally, he is the type of guy who blames everything on something or someone else. We see rampant examples of this type in our political landscape, the world of entertainment, and the circle of grown males of power and influence in general. The most surreal irony is that often the only time of peace in a grown male's life is the time when his inner "firestarter" is absent.

This book will further define the differences between grown males and *Men* walking in manhood. The heart-wrenching reality is that *Men*, all too often, get lumped into one category. So we need a breakdown between the simple existence of grown males and the specific ingredients needed to make a *Man*.

It's going to be an entertaining, emotional, and educational journey, but I truly believe it will be worth every minute. Let's go!

CHAPTER 1

WHAT IS A *MAN?*

All too often, some of the most critical aspects of our lives require absolutely no formal training—marriage and parenting, for example. You do not have to take a class to become a parent or even to marry someone, even though these are both lifelong commitments. No formal training is required for these monumental tasks, and unfortunately many of us do not even seek out information that would be beneficial to us. The impact of these decisions will be significantly felt by all participants and will affect their overall quality of life for years to come.

If a *"Man* University" existed, the class that would be taught to qualify a male for marriage, parenting, and family life in general would be called Manhood 101. I can hear every woman who is reading this book breathe a deep sigh of relief as she vigorously rubs her hands together in anticipation! And that's simply because for far too long, women have had to bear the infirmities of grown males who never matriculated into manhood. (I'll explain the "grown male" concept in greater detail as we go.) For now, let me briefly talk about the word *matriculate* and why I constantly use it in describing the process that a male goes through in maturing into his manhood.

Merriam-Webster's definition for *matriculate* is "to enroll as a member of a body and especially of a college or university." To enroll in anything is a choice. And a male has to choose to enroll in the body of manhood, which will in turn mature him into a

Man. Additionally, this book will also serve as a metaphorical university aimed at providing a foundation for manhood. So when I say "matriculate into manhood," I'm referring to the choice we all, as males, make to dedicate ourselves to *earning* the title of *"Man."* I want to stress here that we have to earn the title, not just have it freely given to us because we reach a certain age.

Now, let's take a hypothetical stroll on the campus of *"Man* University." Let's pretend for a moment that I have been appointed as the president of this institution of higher learning and that I am also the professor for the Manhood 101 course. In university terms, this course would not be considered an elective. This indeed would be a required course for both grown males and *Men* alike.

I would begin my first lecture by explaining to the class that it is our mission here at *Man* U to turn males into *Men*—to elevate *Men* to their highest degree of manhood—and if women were to audit this class, to teach them how to readily identify a *Man* in order to avoid dating or marrying merely a grown male. Our very first Manhood 101 lecture would cover information that can be found within the biblical story of Jesus Christ. To drive home the point, I would set up my projector and drop the screen down so that the students could see Christ modeling the example that all *Men* should mirror: *service over self.*

Paul the apostle once identified Jesus as the ultimate example of servant leadership.[1] Far be it from me to disagree with the apostle on that. Christ is the embodiment of God, or you might say, "God in the flesh." His life clearly reminds me that we were destined to embody the same qualities and purpose when we were created. In fact, Christ is my daily standard and the mechanism that steadies my course.

THE FIRST MALE

I'm further reminded of my shortcomings and my susceptibility to them as I examine the Bible's story of Adam in the Garden of Eden.[2] God had given Adam explicit instructions that specifically explained which trees he could eat from and which ones he couldn't. Many people see Eve's offering of the fruit to Adam as unfortunate and blame her for Adam's failure. I am not one of those people. I deeply believe that Adam couldn't clearly see who he was as a man without the fruit, so he allowed his flesh to indulge. While he accepted it from Eve, I can imagine he did so because he was looking for something or someone to serve as his scapegoat in order to feed his need. While this may have been *Adam's* problem, it has become problematic throughout the history of mankind.

As I alluded to earlier, many people have drawn the conclusion from the text that the woman, in this case, Eve, is the "weaker vessel," or simply weaker than her counterpart, her husband, Adam.[3] It has been my observation that women generally are emotional first. The many women I have encountered in more than a half century of life make me convinced this is accurate. These women include my mother, my grandmother (may she rest in peace), my wife, and my daughter—to name just a few. But again, that's generally speaking. *Men*, generally speaking, are physical first. (We will certainly explore the potential for peril or peace in these differences later.) All that being considered, a *Man* must demonstrate that he is the "stronger vessel" by resisting anything that would lead him to become over-emotional or inappropriately physical. A *Man* must make decisions out of an accumulation of facts and a logical application of them.

As previously promised, let's cover the difference between being a *Man* and being a male.

My son, in these years of his adolescence, often finds himself asking his mom for anything and everything he could otherwise get for himself. She and I could be sitting in close proximity to one another, but he always makes a beeline for my wife. "Mom, can you get me some grapes?" "Mom, can you get me something to drink?" "Mom, Mom, Mom . . ." Why is that? Simple! He knows she will serve him, no matter the request. My son, despite my daily example of manhood, is in the midst of maleness. That's acceptable right now because he's a boy who lacks the full development of the prefrontal cortex a male typically possesses. The prefrontal cortex is the region of the brain used for complex cognitive behavior, personality expression, decision making, and moderation of social behavior.

The book of 1 Corinthians reminds us, "When I was a child, I talked like a child, I thought like a child, I reasoned like a child. When I became a man, I put the ways of childhood behind me."[4] The ways of grown males are usually those of a child, and children constantly want to be served. My son knows I would have him do things for himself whenever possible, not because I don't love him or because I don't serve him as well. I do love him; however, my job is to get him to learn how to serve himself as he prepares to become a godly servant who ultimately begins to serve others.

When we enable a boy, we disable a Man.

With anything we want to become good at, we have to be diligent about doing the appropriate amount of "reps" (practice). In other words, my job is to make sure he gets practice at being self-sufficient. I often say, "When we enable a boy, we disable a *Man*." As his manhood drill instructor, I am responsible, further, to keep drilling home the ways of a *Man* so that when he is no longer an adolescent, he will be prepared to matriculate into manhood. However, it is vitally important for him to complete his boyhood *first*. Completing his boyhood allows him to elevate his mind and spirit in a timely fashion.

MOTH TO A FLAME

Boys who come from an environment that would like them to be responsible enough and strong enough to be a *Man* are often urged to act like one without the necessary skill sets to be one. They sometimes come from backgrounds where the father is missing or inactive in the home, and a *Man* supplement is needed. The pressure to act like a *Man* can cause the kind of trauma to a boy that scars him and scares him out of ever getting prepared to be a *Man*.

When a boy is told he is the "*Man* of the house" (or MOTH), simply because no other males are present, it is often confusing and frustrating. Many young males in my neighborhood who had absent fathers were given the MOTH title because no other male was present, and many of them never recovered from it. Think about how traumatizing it was for them to be given a title and expectations that they did not possess the skill sets to fulfill. As the MOTH, devoid of the power to make any key decisions about the direction of the household or the tools to formulate them, and frequently chastised by their female parent, many of my friends were left feeling powerless in the place they called home, often viewing the woman of the house as someone they would be in battle with and not in partnership with.

This is a common phenomenon that rarely gets examined. The MOTH is assigned to a house that will burn him due to the flames—the fires that often flare up in unbalanced households. His mother has dubbed him a "*Man*" but will shame him for not performing like one in the hopes that it will activate him to become one. (Rarely does it ever happen.) It leaves many of our brothers feeling as though they will never be able to live up to the title of "*Man*" because no one ever explained that manhood isn't an age or a title that someone gives you to fill a void; rather, it is a collection of skill sets and a dedication to service.

When boys are forced to abandon their boyhood because they've been told to "act like a *Man*," they simply become actors, pretenders, in the ways of manhood. And just as a gentle reminder, this "acting" usually happens when a mother who has no *Man* in the home needs to have a functioning male helper to contribute to the inner workings of the house. Some moms think that if they give their son the title of *Man*, it will magically activate it. This is how boyhood gets stolen from young boys trying to become the *Men* who are missing from their families. One can compile a long list of pop singers, athletes, actors, and high-profile people in general who were forced to abandon their boyhood to "act like a man" or be the MOTH. The effects are catastrophic and usually irreversible.

WHAT IS A *MAN*?

We now come to the cream of the crop. *Man*! A grown male and a *Man* are polar opposites. They are like magnets with the same pole that repel and oppose each other. A male who is grown is stuck in the mentality of a boy and generally looks to be served. A *Man*, simply put, is a male who generally looks to be of service.

Let's pause for a minute and let that sink in.

A male seeks *to be served*; a *Man* seeks *to be of service*.

These two entities could not be more opposite. A *Man* is the "industry standard" of males. He is the standard-bearer who covers every woman and child in his life. Notice that I didn't state that he covers *only* his woman and his children. A *Man* is a walking "tree" that provides proper cover from all of the elements in the world that bring harm to his village or his tribe. His daily mission is to choose service over self and deny his flesh that is looking to derail and betray him. Manhood is not finite. There are levels to it.

A male seeks to be served; a Man seeks to be of service.

Manhood is like a martial art. Even when you've learned to like your manhood, there are higher and higher degrees of it that you should seek to achieve. In martial arts, most people are trying to achieve the rank of a black belt. However, the black belt is not the destination. It simply becomes a small portion of the journey. There are first-degree black belts, second-degree, third-degree, and so on. There are even grand masters. Many males give up on the practice of manhood because the pursuit of it, much like a martial art, is endless. Becoming a *Man* is the expectation of every male who is ever born! Unfortunately, some never get the information necessary to achieve *Man* status, while many never actually apply the information they do receive.

But I digress. Meanwhile, back at *Man* U, I will pick up my lecture by writing one word on the board, one that I mentioned earlier...

ACCOUNTABILITY

Men take responsibility for their actions and for the actions of those who follow their leadership. Even if a *Man* is not to blame for a problem, he is willing to take responsibility for addressing it. Healing it. Covering it. A *Man* has the courage to make decisions based on good information, is always willing to be wrong and say so when he is, and, finally, says to himself daily, "I am the problem, and I am the solution."

A *Man* should see himself as the solution or as a contribution to a solution in all situations. If he is not the solution, then he must accept that he has become a part of the problem. He must be willing to be transparent. A *Man* must always be willing to submit himself to God's direction as he seeks clarity. Admitting when we are wrong indicates to those around us that they are truly in the company of leadership. It lets them know we are human and capable of making mistakes. Furthermore, it lets them know they are safe from being blamed and shamed when we are wrong, and that we will take responsibility when the ship is heading in the wrong direction.

Since a *Man* has to avoid blaming and shaming, he must be willing to shoulder all of the responsibility—even when he knows that others may have contributed to the circumstances he now faces. In other words, he may not be to blame, but he does have to accept responsibility. For instance, I have often said to my younger brothers about marriage, "You better get used to taking responsibility for your marriage, because if it doesn't work, everyone will simply ask, 'What did *he* do wrong?'"

A *Man* should always take responsibility for things in order to model the behaviors of a leader that can be mirrored by his house and community. And I can hear the pundits now. "Are you saying that women can't lead?" Absolutely not! But this book is about manhood because a lack of it has been a problem in our culture and has severely crippled our society, preventing us from being truly united. Historically, women have not been the problem. But neither have their counterparts—*Men. Grown males* have been, and continue to be, society's pervasive problem. (More on this in the next chapter.)

One of my best friends—my business partner and accountability partner, Hasani Pettiford—always says, "Every *Man* needs a *Man*." We need it for loving accountability—the kind of accountability that will not make provisions that allow most males to slip through the cracks of development. Hasani and I are intentional about listening to each other's struggles, offering practical solutions, and then holding each other to account—for everything from our marriage and children to our personal and professional goals and even our health. We speak hard truths to each other, accompanied by unwavering respect.

This is what I meant when I referred to "loving accountability." Hasani might say, "Dré, I think you should have a deeper conversation with your wife about this." Or I might say, "H, you need to spend more quality time with the family." Either way, we honor each other as partners in leadership. We both know how difficult it is to walk out our assignments as fathers, husbands, friends, mentors, servants—as *Men*.

Spiritually, mentally, emotionally, and physically, we have to seek our wellness. A *Man* has to be conscious of these four areas and pursue perfection in them. Now I hope you read that sentence carefully. I didn't say he had to be perfect. I said he has to "pursue perfection." We are not perfect, and we never will be. However, what we can do consistently is pursue perfection.

To pursue perfection spiritually, mentally, emotionally, and physically is to ensure that you are an authentic, thriving *Man*. If manhood were a recipe, these would be the big "four at the core" of the secret sauce (with all due respect to responsibility and accountability, of course). They render us helpless or hopeful psychologically, socially, and sexually. These areas dictate how we show up in our relationships, family life, workplace, and community. They inform the way we deal with any and all things.

I know that was a lot! If you got lost in my academic delivery and you can take away only one thought from this chapter, it should be this: generally, a grown male looks to be served, while a *Man* looks *to be of service.*

We have talked about how a *Man* must have responsibility and accountability. We further have touched on seeking wellness spiritually, mentally, emotionally, and physically. But in order to be a *Man*, you also must have instruction.

DENY YOUR DISTRACTION WITH DISCIPLED BROTHERS

I previously mentioned that I am my son's manhood drill instructor. I give him the information that's necessary, and then I drill the application of that information into him. Now while you may be older than my adolescent son, you should always have people in your life who can provide you with information and check you, if necessary.

Trust me, I am not talking to you about anything that I have not experienced. My life went to another level the minute I welcomed discipled brothers into my life—brothers who could speak truth to me. Hasani and others like him love me enough to call me out on my mess, and now I do the same for them.

There are so many individuals (both men and women) who

never ascend to the level of greatness intertwined within their DNA because they get caught up in a distraction that has derailed their destiny. Please hear me. Don't cheat on your destiny with your distraction. The level of success you can achieve if you just remain focused and deny your distraction (your flesh) is exponential.

"Denying your distraction" (again, your flesh) is something I am teaching my son right now. I am using both academics and athletics to illustrate the possibilities of his potential and the depths of his responsibilities every day. I tell him almost daily that he has two jobs: school and sports. And his responsibility is to take care of those as diligently as I take care of making sure he gets a great school experience and an equally great sports experience. I use academics and athletics to help me train my son in the ideals of manhood—work ethic, teamwork, collaboration, cooperation, effort, energy, and focus.

Now I know some of you may be saying, "Aren't you stealing his boyhood?" There's a delicate balance we have to achieve in allowing our boys to complete their boyhood while introducing responsibility and information that will allow them to smoothly transition into manhood. I try to remember that if I *enable* the boy in my son now (immaturity, dependence), I *disable* the *Man* in him later. I believe a KID is really a King In Development. That has to come with appropriate amounts of information and responsibility that prepare him for his next phase in life.

I often hear about and sometimes witness sisters who have a *Man* in their son's life but who still try to teach their son manhood without the *Man*'s contribution. I think this kind of approach does the son a disservice by not allowing critical instruction from that *Man*. Remember, iron sharpens iron.[5] Paternal direction and training are prerequisites to matriculating into manhood because manhood is not a destination. It does not automatically kick in at the age of eighteen or twenty-one. Your son's ability to grow a beard, his ability to procreate, and his deepening voice will not make him a *Man*. He needs proper instruction. Identify the *Man* or *Men* (we all know at least one) in your life whom you trust to help you make sure your son gets the lessons he needs.

Women often ask me what they can do to get their son to be a *Man*. Unequivocally, I say, "Nothing!" Your job is done. You cannot teach him to be something you are not! You can do a great deal for him, like teaching him key principles of manhood—to be polite, to open doors and pull out chairs, to have self-respect, to hold to the value of a woman, to practice godliness and good hygiene, and so forth. But you cannot teach him how to be a *Man*.

For example, every gangster or hardened criminal I have ever spoken with about his parents (and there have been many) has expressed great love and/or respect for his mother. Each one has conveyed endearing feelings toward his mother and admitted that she "did her best." Now if they all felt that way about their mothers but all shared the fact that they were fatherless (some can be fatherless while their father is actually living in the house), this feeling gives us a very clear idea that women are not the key ingredient to manhood.

Boys need to be fathered, not necessarily by their biological father, but they do need to be fathered. Boys who go unfathered often wind up being fathered by the state. And the state knows only one way of fathering: it locks them up. I know this seems like harsh talk, but it is the real talk we need to begin having so that we don't perpetuate the epidemic of gang violence, incarceration, and premature death that we are currently experiencing.

One of the reasons you are so tired, my sister, is that you live in a world that tells you that you "don't need a *Man*." Well, I want to correct that. You don't need another child to raise; you don't need a grown *male* who depends on you to pay his bills. Now if you are helping each other, that is another story, but that's not what I am talking about; I am talking about the brother who lives in *your* house, eats *your* food, drives *your* car, and uses all *your* gas. That dude is a straight firestarter—the kind who sets everything and everyone on fire, based on his own deficits. This kind is what you will have on your hands if you can't identify the difference between a male and a *Man*. Or this is what you will raise if you don't choose to allow a *Man* to speak life into your son's existence.

I recently heard a controversial statement made by a prominent individual who publicly acknowledged how much he loved his wife because she stood by his side and covered him until he matriculated into manhood. Well, ladies, I am telling you right now—ten years is a long time to be a grown male's mother when you're supposed to be his wife. It is not your job to be broken and sad while the grown male in your life denies or too slowly acknowledges that he isn't fulfilling his manhood destiny.

This yoke is just not God's will for your life. Life is too short for you to be feeling depressed, stalking your guy, approaching other females about him (don't ever do that again), following him in your friend's car, going through his phone and his browser history! If you have to do that, then you have just acknowledged that you are probably not with a *Man*. (You may also be acknowledging that you might be more female than woman. But that's a topic for my next book.) A lack of manhood causes great devastation, especially to the women who participate in that kind of behavior.

WINNING THE
BATTLE OF THE FLESH

The last portion of my lecture at *Man* U would cover winning the battle of the flesh. Paul the apostle (what can I say . . . I like the guy) writes in the book of Romans, "Our old self was crucified with him [Jesus] in order that the body of sin might be brought to nothing."[6] When Paul uses the phrase "the body of sin," he's talking about the flesh. The flesh and the Spirit are diametrically opposed to each other. The Spirit is the Holy Spirit, whom God certainly put in us to serve as the great navigator who would order our steps. The flesh, which is really being driven by the world, is the thing that gets us further away from God's intended path for our life. Therefore, every day, my job as a *Man* is to deny the flesh (selfish pursuits and desires) in order to allow the Spirit to guide my steps.

My job is to hear the inner monologue of the Spirit that says, "You are a powerful *Man* who has been sent here to be a servant leader." Will it be service or self? The "service" is of my spirit, while the "self" is of my flesh. Winning the battle of my service versus my self is the daily fight of every *Man* who chooses not to be the male that society enables him to be. Dr. Maya Angelou (may she rest in peace) said, "Do the best you can until you know better. Then when you know better, do better."[7] Well, she was speaking to a different era. During that time, we didn't know better because we had limited access to information—no wholesome talk shows, no podcasts, no audiobooks, no web surfing, no blogs, no smartphones. She was asking us to do the best we could with what we

> *My job as a* Man *is to deny the flesh in order to allow the Spirit to guide my steps.*

WHAT IS A MAN?

didn't have! We now have all of these resources at our disposal, and we're still not doing any better.

Well, I say, with all due respect to our queen Maya Angelou, that we set the stage to do better when we *choose* better. We are more likely to do better because we have acquired information, or at least *access* to information. But it doesn't stop there. We have to *choose better.* As *Men*, we have to choose better about all of the things that get us into trouble, the things of male irresponsibility that the flesh is trying to engulf us in—dishonesty, infidelity, hypocrisy, jealousy, pornography, and chemical dependency. These pitfalls all too frequently cause us to abandon our posts with our women and children because it is easier to be a male than it is to be a *Man.* Truthfully speaking, the only things you need are a penis and a pulse. But to be a *Man* you need to have purpose and precision. And all of that is a choice. We were built to win our battles and make the best choices because we were constructed by the Most High in his glorious reflection.[8] We know that winning the battle of the flesh is the first step to becoming a grand master in manhood.

Again, there is a huge difference in being a male versus a *Man.* I am a *Man.*

CHAPTER 2

WHAT IS A MALE?

certainly hope you enjoyed your time with me at *Man* U. It is an excellent institution for higher manhood learning, so we will revisit the campus periodically during our time together. The next stop on our journey leads us to Life Experience Studios, where I have been appointed the executive in charge of programming. The content we will feature in this chapter is that of a reality show. While I don't watch any reality shows, just because my life is real enough, it is helpful for me to use them as a device for the sake of clarity. This show is called *The Grown Males of Anytown, USA* (*TGM*). The characters of *TGM* are based on people and situations I have encountered in my many years of life as a male—but, more importantly, as a *Man*.

The characters are five lifelong friends who have many similar circumstances, but tragically the lowest common denominator is undoubtedly the most pivotal of them all. The show highlights the mind-sets, strengths, and weaknesses of grown males. As I have already explained, the true nature of a grown male is to be served—much to the detriment of most, and beneficial to very few. Let's meet the stars of the show, and I'm confident you will see what I mean.

First is Antonio, affectionately known to the fellas as "Tone." He is a thirty-eight-year-old policeman, married with no children. Then there is Oliver, known to the crew as "O." He is forty-five, twice married, with an adult child along with an eight-year-old.

Next meet Ralph. This twenty-nine-year-old, fourth-generation plumber who loathes the family business is a recovering alcoholic and is separated from his wife. Now meet fifty-two-year-old Russell, who is a retired military officer–turned–local politician, married with two children. Lastly, Stanley is a twenty-six-year-old retired overseas basketball player. He has nine children with almost as many mothers.

I am sure you are saying to yourself, *That is quite an assortment of characters.* The truth is, we've only scratched the surface of who these guys are. This reality show, like all of the truly sensationalized ones, will uncover the ugly details. But unlike most, we will point out the layers that formulated their personalities and led to their arrested development, and what cemented their Peter Pan state of being. I will describe in full detail many of the characteristics that comprise the DNA of the grown male. So now back to our regularly scheduled programming.

ANTONIO

Our thirty-eight-year-old policeman, Antonio, has worked hard to achieve the rank of sergeant. He typically handles tremendous responsibilities on his shifts and oversees the training of other officers. He is a great leader and is well respected by most of the force. He has the potential to become a captain one day. He is a perfectionist and suffers from obsessive-compulsive disorder (OCD), which makes him exceptional in managing the details of any operation. However, the same traits that make him thrive at work wreak havoc in most of his other relationships. He pushes every woman away because he is comparing them to his mother, who still cooks his meals and does his grocery shopping. She is overly critical of every woman he has ever cared about, and he refuses to move forward in a relationship without her approval.

Antonio never knew his father. His parents had him while they were still in high school, and his father went into the military upon graduation and was killed in active duty.

Antonio and his mother were very poor when he was growing up and had little in the way of material possessions, so his mother was constantly cleaning the house and rearranging the few things they did have. Antonio grew up with that same restlessness, which now presents itself in the form of OCD. His mother did date while he was growing up, but she refused to let any of the men she dated discipline or hold Antonio accountable. Ironically, as a result of growing up without a *Man*'s accountability, Tone has always had a chip on his shoulder and actually rebelled against men—unless it directly benefited him to submit to another man's leadership, as in the case of his career as a policeman.

Tone not only rebels against men but often lashes out at them. He has developed the skill to appear to respect the leadership and authority of other men but will often do things his own way as a sort of silent protest. This characteristic appears all too often with grown males. Because they were never taught to submit to male leadership, they are unable to be fully accountable to another *Man*.

This inability to submit to other men affects them in many ways. For one, it stunts their development because they can only accept counsel from women, and they usually don't do that very well unless it comes from their own mother. This creates an imbalance in their lives and becomes an even bigger issue when a *Man*'s perspective is necessary. Other problems that are evident and preventing Tone from matriculating into manhood are his stunted areas of growth as a husband and father. He discontinues any romantic relationship before it gets too serious because he loathes the idea of the permanent responsibility of a family. Without an intervention, Tone may continue to be an accomplished police officer, but he will not develop a healthy, sustainable, or successful relationship.

OLIVER

Oliver is the CEO of a multimillion-dollar publishing company started by his father, and he has been married twice. What makes his story tragic is that he sacrificed his first family to make the business thrive.

Like Antonio, Oliver's dad passed away as well, and the business was nearly bankrupt when he did. "O" was able to make the company profitable by bringing it into the twenty-first century with sharp ideas and rebranding. His coolness in the office belied his nerd-like existence in school; he never received much attention from the ladies. So, of course, he was excited when his shy wife, Cheryl, had agreed to go out with him back in college. They became best friends and subsequently inseparable.

At the time, O's father had openly disapproved of him getting "so serious so soon," because he felt Oliver should have taken more of his path—join a fraternity and, as the saying goes, "sow his wild oats." Oliver had seen the emotional distress his father inflicted on his mother over the years due to countless affairs and, even more egregiously, having a second family in another part of the state. O vowed that he would never live a life like his father's. But the success of the business, the influx of power, and the temptations that came with it were more than Oliver could resist. He soon found himself entangled in a relationship with one of his publishing clients, and that relationship produced a child.

Cheryl and Oliver's son, David, were devastated by his actions, and David decided he did not want to have a relationship with Oliver. Lastly, and more painfully, David decided he no longer wanted Oliver's last name. Cheryl and David subsequently moved to another state. O now sees his son only on certain holidays.

The relationship that broke up his marriage was short-lived also. O and his mistress soon married after the divorce from Cheryl, but it failed to last even two years. Their daughter, Ivory, is the best thing that came out of the relationship, but his infidelity has put that relationship in jeopardy as well. As a pattern and practice, he was caught cheating with one of his employees. At forty-five years old, O is proof that an MBA and a multimillion-dollar entity don't equate to success, happiness, or even peace.

RALPH

Our third player, no pun intended, is Ralph. While on scholarship at a major university, Ralph was an all-American quarterback touted as the "best of the best" by his sophomore year. Professional teams were poised to offer him lucrative deals when he was done with college, but an ACL injury during his junior year changed everything. Unable to successfully rehab his injury and feeling depressed, Ralph began abusing substances and alcohol to cope with the change in his life's trajectory. His addictions made him more uncaring and irresponsible and got him quickly expelled from school and sent back home.

Ralph never recovered from his change of status—from future

national athlete hero to local average zero. At twenty-nine years old, he loathed his new future: going into the family business—plumbing. His dad was long gone before he was born, choosing to opt out of responsibility for a newborn child. Despite not having his dad around, his granddad and uncles (his mom's brothers), who were all plumbers, taught him the family trade when he was young. He grew up resenting his dad for leaving and the men in his life for selecting a trade that had them dealing with other people's—how should I say this?—poop.

His high school sweetheart, Lorna, had been with him through all his super highs and mega lows. They eventually married, and she was even inspired to become an addiction counselor to better understand Ralph and "stand by her man." However, when his anger and frustration turned into violent encounters between the two of them, she packed his things and, with the assistance of the police, had him removed. She even got a restraining order from the courts. As with his knee injury, the damage to his marriage seems irreparable. He will undoubtedly be arrested if he attempts to return home. His firstborn child may even be aborted due to his wife feeling alone, unsafe, and uncovered.

RUSSELL

On the surface, Russell has it all together. There are no mistresses, no second families, but that's only because Russell knows those things are bad for his image. The fifty-two-year-old's political ambitions are everything to him. Russell is obsessed with power; as a matter of fact, he will do anything to achieve and retain it. You see, Russell's dad was a hustler. He hustled women and cards, and he was rumored to have "disposed" of a few bodies as well. Known to do anything for money and the accumulation of it, he taught Russell the art of the deal before it became a book.

Russell learned the ways of a con man and how to morph into any person he needed to become to get what he wanted—at any cost! However, he has a secret. Russell is gay. He does not act on his impulses because he must be in character at all times. He has carefully been wearing this mask since one of his dad's friends started molesting him. His dad would have the friend over from time to time, and he was like an uncle to Russell. The friend often came over after one of their hustles, and from time to time, his dad had this friend watch Russell when a sitter was necessary.

When Russell told his mom of the sexual encounter, she presented the accusation to his dad. He became so angry that they got into a huge argument. Refusing to believe the account or accept responsibility for not properly vetting his friend and protecting his family, Russell's dad took him aside and told him, "Never mention that story again. Time heals all wounds if we don't bring them up."

The incident would leave his parents' already somewhat dysfunctional relationship untenable. His dad made appearances in Russell's life just to keep up the facade, but the family was broken, and Russell grew up without a *Man* to guide him.

On Russell's twelfth birthday, his mom hosted a few of his friends for a sleepover. During the sleepover, one of the boys came over to where Russell was sleeping and began touching him and eventually orally copulated him. Bizarrely he felt dirty but was aroused all at once. It is extremely difficult for a child to process events like this and to find clarity within. He decided to take his father's advice and not say anything to his mother so that, yet once again, time would "heal all wounds."

As you can well imagine, wounds like this do not heal with time alone. Russell walked around with his burden for years, and his encounters with this boy and his father's friend began to inform his sexuality. (It doesn't work this way for everyone, but in Russell's case it did.) The shame he carried in feeling like less of a *Man* for being the victim in these encounters was outweighed by the necessity to speak his grief and pain. He subsequently joined the military to prove he was "manlier" than any of his friends. He eventually got married and even had two children to live up to what he thought his constituents would expect from their male public servant.

STANLEY

Finally, we have twenty-six-year-old Stanley. Stanley was raised in a house with his mom, grandmother, two aunts, four female cousins, and his mom's live-in boyfriend. He was the first boy in their family in three generations, so he was continuously spoiled. It was rumored that his dad was a married professional athlete, but his mom would never talk about it, no matter how much Stanley pressed or his grandmother urged.

However, his mom made sure he never went without anything. She worked two jobs, and he was often left with his grandmother, aunts, and cousins because the boyfriend was not there to raise "someone else's child." He was simply there to have a relationship with the mom and saw Stanley only as a burden.

When Stanley showed an aptitude for sports, his mother spared no expense to send him to camps and buy him the best training gear. It paid off in a mighty way. The DNA that he inherited from his unconfirmed father, along with the support of his mother in supplying his dreams with instruction and accountability for his chosen sport, turned into a lucrative career in Europe.

While not in the NBA, he was still making a couple million dollars a year playing the game he loved. It afforded him great material resources, as well as great sexual conquests. As a young teen, he quickly understood that if his skills on the court grew like he was growing physically, he would get plenty of attention from the opposite sex, which he never turned down. Unfortunately, he did not realize his insatiable need for attention from women would be his downfall. Stanley was procreating with the same success rate as his shooting percentage. He had nine children, once having two in a year, with eight different women. His child support payments and extravagant lifestyle would have landed him in the poorhouse had he not gotten strategic legal advice to protect some of his assets.

Stanley's chronic irresponsibility and charming personality have created a train wreck lifestyle. He has great difficulty trying to be a father to his six sons and three daughters. His go-to parenting move is to buy the girls what they want with the limited resources he has at his disposal. This is specifically upsetting to the mothers of the sons, who show up to remind him of his unfulfilled responsibilities, as well as his lack of "manhood."

CONCLUSION

Now that you have met all of the characters, let's take a commercial break because I know that was a lot. I hope you see some common themes throughout these story lines. All the males in this show have fathers who were absent or consistently inconsistent. The males who were in their lives were either unable to have a positive impact or were merely a toxic influence that further perpetuated maleness. No male will mature into a *Man* or be capable of being a father without first being fathered.

While these characters are all semi-fictional, the people they represent are genuine. In fact, we may know a few of them personally. Wait a minute. On second thought, we *all* know some males like this. The challenge we face in our culture is that the grown male is a product of our making, and the cycle of dysfunction that currently exists keeps all grown males spinning on the hamster wheel of maleness—vigorously moving but not making any forward progress. In an article written by Thorgil Bjornson, we learn that "nearly eighty percent of teachers are female. Over forty percent of boys are raised by single mothers. This means that nearly half of boys grow up with mostly, or *entirely* feminine influence at home and school."[1]

> "Nearly half of boys grow up with mostly, or *entirely* feminine influence at home and school."

Think about this for a minute. Looking at these statistics, it's no wonder we have a crisis of "grown males" among every race, class, and culture. There are not enough men* around to demonstrate what manhood looks like. Have you ever wondered how this epidemic became so bad? Let's discuss a few reasons.

#1—Kids' Sports and Political Correctness

When I grew up, there were winners and losers. It was okay to lose; it meant that you, like all of us, had some more work to do.

---

* I almost used the term "real men" to drive home the point, but I hate that term. If this book teaches you anything, it should be that you are either a *Man* or a male. There's no such thing as a "real man." Either you are a *Man*, or you are not!

You had to practice harder and practice better to beat the other guy or the other team. I'm not sure when it happened, but this era of "everyone is a winner so let's give everyone a medal" is challenging for children in general, but young boys especially. *Men* know that it takes being better, stronger, and faster to have the mind-set to compete and win in the real world.

Where I grew up in Brooklyn, you understood that if you lost in a pickup basketball game, you were going to get roasted indefinitely and have to wait for a while to play again due to the number of people waiting to get on the court. It made you work hard to win. It drove me and my friends, because we had no desire to watch other guys play while we waited for our next opportunity. Now I'm not saying we have to "roast" our boys or expose them to demeaning behavior, but we are certainly eliminating the aspects that count the most: truth, accountability, and perspective. These clear components are missing from the childhoods of young males and preventing them from matriculating into manhood.

#2—Lack of Rites of Passage Signifying Moving from Boyhood to Manhood

In Western civilization, rites of passage are pretty much nonexistent. One such practice in Africa was hunting lions, for example. According to the Maasai Association, "Lion hunt was a tradition and historical practice that played an important role in the Maasai culture. The practice was different from trophy hunting; it was symbolically a rite of passage rather than a hobby."[2] And when the men took the boys who were coming into their manhood, they separated them from their mothers for weeks so that the mother wouldn't be able to protect the boy from acts that would be painful but necessary for his growth. We cannot grow a male into a *Man* while he is in the space of accommodation, convenience, and comfort.

We must begin to create and implement some modern-day rites of passage for our boys that signal to their minds and spirits that they are beginning to matriculate into manhood. These things should be a focus not of masculinity but of manhood, which has *service* at the core of it—for instance, taking a boy out into the community to serve the homeless, to help women who are unpartnered, to serve the needs of children who have fewer resources.

We cannot grow a male into a Man while he is in the space of accommodation, convenience, and comfort.

These things can become great modern-day rites of passage that will serve as the necessary activation mechanisms for matriculating our boys into manhood.

#3—Parents' Obsession with Protecting Their Children from *Everything*

As a result of this obsession, we have a generation of entitled individuals with "failure to thrive." Medically speaking, according to Children's Hospital of Philadelphia, "failure to thrive is defined as decelerated or arrested physical growth (height and weight measurements fall below the third or fifth percentile, or a downward change in growth across two major growth percentiles) and is associated with abnormal growth and development."[3]

In social terms, Generation Y has failed to thrive in regard to their living situation. In 2016, Pew Research found that for the first time, living at home with parents had become the most common living situation for adults ages eighteen to thirty-four.[4]

Census data suggests that the reality of young adults moving back home is more and more common, and many researchers believe it's a trend that's here to stay, according to an article by Patrick Sisson.[5] Sisson quotes Dr. Jean Twenge, who believes that the housing scenario is part of a larger developmental delay happening with Generation Y and Generation Z:

"The entire developmental pathway has slowed down," she says. "Younger kids aren't given as much independence and responsibility as they used to, and it's taken longer to grow into adulthood."

Those young adults coming after the millennial generation, whom Twenge has called iGen, [are] "putting off adulthood in every way." They're less likely to get a driver's license, date, have sex, and drink alcohol, at the same age as previous generations.

That may seem good on the surface—until you realize these young adults are staying away from *all* "adulting" activities. Now that's not to say that having sex and drinking alcohol will make you an adult. But it is speaking to a bigger issue of us enabling our boys to stay immature, and of them seeking refuge from accountability that nudges them toward their intended destination—*manhood*.

Remember, *when you enable a boy, you disable a Man*.

Now that I have illustrated the various forms that grown males can take and have shown some of the ways this epidemic of immaturity ensues, let's talk about why it is more important than ever to solve these issues so that our young males and grown males can transform into *Men*.

CHAPTER 3

CALM IN CHAOS

As we depart the studios and bid the production team farewell, I have yet another artistic presentation for you back on the campus of *Man* U. Every year, the theater department has a talent show. We won't stay for the entire show, but there is one young man I want you to experience. His stage name is CIC. It stands for "Calm in Chaos." He was one of the first students to take the Manhood 101 class. For his final project, he's created a spoken word piece called "Calm in Chaos," which is how he got his name. He creates poetry based on his transformation from a grown male to a *Man*. CIC told the class that he knew he was actually a *Man* when he began to function in a state of calmness more than a state of chaos and could introduce calm into spaces of chaos or calamity.

I saved you a seat. We are just in time to hear CIC rock the mic.

Lights dim. Spotlight flashes on. CIC enters center stage wearing all black with the spotlight hitting only his face. The lighting, along with the black effect, makes his face seem to be suspended in midair. CIC begins spoken word:

Once there was a storm that brewed deep within me,
a chaos I could not control and a calm I could not see.
The least little tribulation would set me into hyperventilation
due to the violent nature of my latest iteration.

I would misappropriate the women who truly were a blessing;

to be godly honest, I adored the beefing and the stressing.

Allergic to responsibility, wanting no accountability,

my manhood seemed far beyond my male-like visibility.

"Male in chaos" described me as a loss,

sewn into my being as if I was quilted by Betsy Ross.

Then one night, through the Salt and the Light,

God asked if I was ready. I said, "Maybe, I might."

He said like Christ I could be calm and be free

from all the pain that was diligent in tormenting me.

In need of prayer, I cannot be delivered on my own;

I'm turned around like "flesh of my flesh and bone of my bones."

Through a spiritual consignment, I am a *Man* newly in alignment;

the intention of my creation is my purpose and assignment.

From the ways of a child there is a lifelong ban;

I am calm in chaos, matriculating from a male to a *Man*.

CIC bows. The spotlight fades to total blackness. The crowd cheers.

Wow. I don't know about you, but as a recovering grown male, I find those words to be a powerful description of the emotions I felt *constantly*. I said "recovering grown male" because, like any addict, I have to acknowledge my addiction to my flesh and to things that make me feel good but leave others feeling bad.

The thing about living in a state of chaos is that you don't control it; it controls you. Chaos is an equal opportunity oppressor. It doesn't care whether you are of color or Caucasian, accomplished or not, rich or poor. As a matter of fact, if you don't learn to control chaos, not only will it control you, but it will slowly begin to break you down.

LESSONS FROM UFC

I want to tell you a story about a UFC fight. I won't give you the names of the combatants, because I don't want either male to be categorized and forever memorialized as a grown male. And I want us all to remember that our job is not to judge anyone; rather, we should, whenever possible, avoid putting others in a position to be judged. Our job here is to observe and assess for the sake of learning and to share the learning for the sake of transformation. With that said, according to the reports, what happened after the fight is a perfect illustration of a grown male creating a space of chaos simply because he could not remain calm.

The story is that a well-known UFC fighter had been doing the prerequisite trash-talking with a great deal of name-calling, causing supreme chaos. The challenger remained calm, however, but was visibly bothered by the champion's statements. There was a struggle going on inside the challenger to remain focused on the task at hand. The day of the fight came. Now, this is where it gets fascinating. The challenger was annoyed and could have retaliated in kind against the champion's childlike tactics. But he chose to remain calm during the fight and won! Many people did not give the challenger a chance, but he beat the chaos-ridden champion into a fourth-round submission. It was a huge victory for him.

This is a lot like the Old Testament story of David and Goliath.[1] Goliath, a champion, was sent by the Philistines to talk trash to Israel. Goliath called out all the warriors of Israel. David, the challenger—just a young shepherd—was like, "Man, you gotta be kidding me! Nobody's gonna deal with this heathen?" Bravely but calmly, David decided to handle it!

Now we all know how that story ends. David, the challenger, beat the champ by knockout via slingshot, and the rest, as they say, is history.

So, to my point, the reigning champion of the UFC fight was the challenger's "Goliath," who talked trash to get under his skin in hopes that the chaos would be distraction enough to help the champion win the fight. But just like David, the challenger in the UFC fight defeated his enemy, and the magnitude of the win should have been the headline of the story. However, life in the messy world of "maleness" is never orderly or neat. Chaos is the home base of most grown males, and they cannot help but try to live comfortably in that space every chance they get.

After the pay-per-view fight was over, fans were treated to a free impromptu one. The fight continued after the match was over because the challenger (the new champion) decided he was going to straighten out the former champion's entire team. He hopped over the cage and into the crowd to exact his punishment on the rest of the opposing corner.

To say he lost it would be an understatement. Under normal circumstances, we would be assessing the physical fallout from such a skirmish. But because of the normally violent nature of the MMA world, most of the participants came away with minor injuries.

But the story doesn't end there, and it isn't that simple. Chaos is not only dangerous and debilitating, but it is contagious. Once the challenger lost his calm, the chaos infected his team, which then infected the former champion and of course infected his team also. Utter pandemonium and ultimate chaos raged inside and outside the caged circle. Subsequently, the challenger's two-million-dollar purse for the fight, which he had just earned by beating the champion, was withheld as a result of his inability to resist the temptation of the flesh—in this case, pride and revenge—and the chaos it produced.

While we may never know the full story of what triggered him and ultimately caused him to tarnish and jeopardize his victory by giving in to his flesh, we do know it was unnecessary. What we also know is this: as *Men*, we have all faced those types of situations that have us locked amid chaos and challenge us to remain calm to navigate the space properly.

We've all encountered situations where someone is trying to goad us or negatively activate us into warrior mode with their language and actions. But we must be calculated about when warrior mode is appropriate. And we must remember we never get points for remaining calm "most of the time." We will only be judged on whether we ultimately gave in to the chaos and opted in to the warrior mode.

Let me be clear: warrior instincts are not all wrong. As calm and as cool as I may be, if someone threatens my family and other loved ones, I can launch into warrior mode in no time flat! Why? Because that is a part of my divine design as a *Man*. God created me to take dominion and establish order.[2] And sometimes we cannot do this with a kind word. Sometimes, in dire situations, we have to use the physicality as a gesture that God gave us to protect ourselves and others who fall under our cover. But let us ask the question, "How often are we truly put in those dire circumstances?"

Even when I lived on the streets of Brooklyn, where, in those pre-gentrification days, I found myself fighting every day, I realized years later that I did not have to succumb to the temptation of my flesh. Most of the time, giving in was a choice. Every exchange that doesn't go our way, every time someone acts out against us, does not have to end dramatically. As *Men*, we have to begin to gracefully exit situations we have outgrown. Usually, we can simply choose to move on to the next chapter in our lives with peace and clarity. But that will never happen unless we are in a space of calm.

As Men, we have to begin to gracefully exit situations we have outgrown.

When I operate in God's image, as he originally intended, which is always in a calm manner, then I create spaces of calm for myself and those around me. When I allow myself to be activated by my flesh and fueled by emotional behavior, I start cycles of chaos for myself and often for those around me—much like the aforementioned MMA fighter. Operating calmly is important for our own spirit, but equally important for the spirit of others because we are supposed to be the models everyone can safely and dependably mirror.

THE POWER OF LANGUAGE

Our language usually plays a huge role in our pain. Language is generally at the center of why we do most things. A trainer for a boxer can activate their fighter to win with the use of language. It is not simply relegated to telling the fighter what he or she is or is not doing, but many times the trainer will use language that gets their fighter to rise to the occasion, motivated to will their way to victory.

This is also true of a teacher who tells a student he or she is capable of being something more than what they currently are. I had a teacher by the name of Ms. Elaine Jackson (may she rest in peace) who often told me I had great talent as a performer and that I was going to "make it" in the entertainment world. Ms. Jackson was so important because she had taught me earlier in life—in my elementary school years—and she actually lived in my neighborhood. Her words of affirmation were hard to come by. Were it not for her words, and of course the words of my mother and my grandmother (may she also rest in peace), I'm confident I would not have made it. Language does something to us or does something for us!

So if language can absolutely activate you, it can likewise deactivate you. The same way I had teachers like Ms. Jackson who affirmed me, I also had teachers who arrested my development with language that discouraged me and played an infomercial of doubts in me for decades. Truthfully, many of those doubts I still battle to this day. I can even remember the teachers' faces, names, and the grades they taught, as far back as my eight-year-old self.

Like Ms. Jackson, I had another teacher in elementary school who told me I was not a very good writer. She said I needed to recognize my strengths and that I had many, but writing was not one of them. That messaging nearly prevented me from writing this book. As a child, you blindly trust that those who are supposed to speak life into your existence will do so. They are the trainers of your young self who are meant to be activators. They are meant to help you set your trajectory in life and inspire you to go higher. While this teacher gave me a compliment by pointing out my strengths, she nearly assassinated the writer in me. If it weren't for my fervent belief that God wanted me to contribute this book as a call to action for manhood, I would have continued to believe my writing was not good enough—that *I* was not good enough.

I have encountered many people like this, as you probably have too. Our job is not to judge them but to observe their behavior and then address the damage they have done. Once we address it, we can become whole and use that experience for the sake of someone else's transformation.

The language of people like this created much chaos in my life. Therefore, I've come up with a great way to identify how chaos is created and how it inflicts pain. Often, chaos is created through pain languages. I am sure many of you are familiar with Gary Chapman's brilliant book *The 5 Love Languages*. Well, I want to share with you my compilation—"The 5 Pain Languages." If I were writing my bible of life, one of the critical chapters would be "The Book of LUCAS." LUCAS is an acronym for my five pain languages:

Lusting = the passion of pain
Unforgivingness = the memory of pain
Cursing = the vocabulary of pain
Anger = the emotion of pain
Sarcasm = the humor of pain

The Book of LUCAS addresses the deficiencies that most of us struggle with and the ways we try to navigate these languages of pain to avoid complete and utter chaos.

When we are kids, we are like pure black slate, not yet stained with powdered white chalk. But children reflect back the truth of their environment with great consistency and accuracy.

One of the first lessons a child learns is that of language. The language spoken to that child and the language spoken over the child's life determine their development and often their trajectory. Generally speaking, we rarely consider just how important language is to people because we usually see them as beings who are capable of managing their ills. But consider this: How many times have you witnessed someone cursing at a newborn baby? Never, right? That would be unthinkably cruel. However, as the child grows, they learn pain languages. When a parent is in pain and begins to communicate to that child in the "vocabulary of pain," they are teaching the child that this is the language that people who love you speak.

Words sting. Words bite. Using language negatively is like injecting a child with "chaos" steroids. Steroids make you bigger, stronger, and more aggressive in the beginning, but they wreak havoc on other parts of your body in the end. Chaos steroids are especially dangerous for males. Negative language teaches them to become master maneuverers in the pain game; it shows them that the way to relieve their pain is to inflict it on others. In other words, rather than deal with my pain, I'll give it to you. This creates environments that are predominately cesspools of pain. In these extreme zones of pain, you feel as though the only way to win is to learn how to crush others with language, ultimately creating chaos in their lives. But a *Man* who is conscious of his life's assignment knows that his language is one of the essential ingredients for a calm environment and a calm human being.

USING THE BEST VOCABULARY

A male's first power is his physicality (remember warrior mode?), but a *Man*'s true power is his vocabulary. His vocabulary is like a ring of keys for a locksmith. Each word holds the potential to unlock something in him or in someone else. His words are like a "protein" that builds someone up rather than a "kerosene" that burns someone down.

Every *Man* is like the firefighter of his home. He is responsible for putting out fires, which creates more calm so that the environment he is in does not turn into a chaotic towering inferno. While his job as a firefighter is to put out fires, he is first responsible for making sure that he himself is not on fire. A *Man* who is on fire will surely be challenged in not setting his own house on fire. As a firefighter, he has to wear flame-retardant clothing on his spirit to avoid being set on fire himself. He knows that if he is set on fire, he may set other people on fire as well. Remember, you are a fire*fighter*; you are not a fire*starter*! Your job is to put fires out, not create them!

Every **Man** *is like the firefighter of his home. He is responsible for putting out fires, which creates more calm and avoids a towering inferno.*

Now you may say to me, "Man, brother, that sounds good, but how in the world do I do that?"

I'm so glad you asked. I am happy to report that it is not something you really can do by yourself. I did not do it by myself. Like any firefighter, I have a team that helps me fight fires. It all begins with reminding myself of God's intention for my life, Christ's example, and my band of brothers who hold me accountable. They all share a few things in common: they all are married (I have very few single friends because most of them want to do single male activities, and those things could negatively influence my walk as a married *Man*); they all have children; and they all believe in God.

That last fact is truly important because we need to have something that is greater than us to help anchor us down. Without something higher than ourselves, we can struggle mightily in the way of humility and accountability. Personally, I am a *Man* of faith. As a born-again believer, I find strength in Jesus Christ. He was a

Man, in the flesh, who sacrificed himself, his very life, for the sake of saving others.

It sounds like Christ was a firefighter too. He is my everyday example of how committed I need to be to my faith and to my life as a *Man*. Christ is the model I mirror, and God is my anchor who keeps me calm and free from chaos. Apart from God, I can do few things great. The message of the Bible is clear that with man, things are impossible, but all things are possible with God.[3] The Bible also says that "the one who is in you is greater than the one who is in the world."[4]

I need God in my life. I cannot maintain the disposition of manhood without him in my life. I cannot express to you what a relief it is to know that I don't have to carry the weight of the responsibilities of husband, father, influencer, and son on my own.

I spend time in God's Word receiving revelation for my life. The Bible is like my firefighting manual. Remember, I'm not selling you on religion; I'm selling you on instruction. The Bible gives me spiritual insights to apply to my life and then disseminate to others. I need to be shown the right way so that I can walk in it. One of my favorite proverbs is found in Proverbs 3:5–6 (TLB): "If you want favor with both God and man, and a reputation for good judgment and common sense, then trust the Lord completely; don't ever trust yourself. In everything you do, put God first, and he will direct you and crown your efforts with success."

When the Bible says "don't ever trust yourself," it means "don't trust your flesh"—the part of you that is flawed and selfish. This is the part of us that has been shaped and informed by the world. It pulls us away from being the perfect design of our Creator. Each time I read that Scripture, it continues to bless me. If you grew up in church, you may have learned it in the NKJV:

Trust in the LORD with all your heart,

And lean not on your own understanding;

In all your ways acknowledge Him,

And He shall direct your paths.

And don't get me wrong, that version is cool too. However, there is something great about a Word that warns me that I need to completely put my trust in God because if I do, I will be someone who has a reputation for good judgment and common sense, which will create opportunities for me to obtain favor with God and *Man*.

Whoa! Let me help you understand how impactful that is to me. I work in an industry where super-talented people go off the deep end and make decisions that damage their reputations. Most of this comes from feeling like they're always in an environment of chaos, unable to feel calm or secure. But God is my measure of security who says, "You're going to prosper, and I will increase you because I love you."

Despite my work environment, my story does not have to be one of chaos and calamity. I have to depend on my faith in God and also work diligently as best I can. Thus we get the Scripture verse, "Faith without works is dead,"[5] and this truth applies to everything in our lives and impacts us all. Faith isn't just asking God for help. That's part of it, but you've got to go out and do the work too. I cannot expect to simply ask God to give me favor and not honor his favor by working as diligently as he worked in creating this earth and giving me life.

Our calm allows us to deal with our pain, which is the chief activator of chaos.

This concept is crucial to me as a *Man*, because I cannot pray and then sit around waiting for God to reward me for doing absolutely nothing. The Living Bible says that if I put God first in everything I do, he will direct me and crown my *efforts* with success. Focus on the word *efforts*. It simply but definitely implies that we have to "do" things along with having faith, and then we will be rewarded. That Scripture is better than a money-back guarantee. It ensures our success. (Remember our definition of success earlier, which is not the same as popular culture's definition.)

This truth takes the pressure off me, since I know that my energy and effort are not isolated and that my Father's promise of a blessed tomorrow will usher me into a place of calm. Our calm allows us to deal with our pain, which is the chief activator of chaos, and will enable us to heal so we don't have to remain mentally and emotionally impaired and imprisoned.

CHAPTER 4

HEALING FOR WHERE IT HURTS

Pain is a touchy subject for most people. It is so touchy that it makes most of us want to run and continue running until we are as far away from accountability as possible. Unfortunately, a lack of accountability leads to a lack of healing or restoration—something we all desperately need. Dealing with pain usually means digging down deep into our souls to access the very things that have shaped who we have become and how we can be healed or restored.

When we arrive on earth as God's creation, we are like a blank slate that has not yet been written on by the choices of others. Each day, each second, we are being affected by the teachings of other imperfect beings who have become flawed by their experiences with yet other imperfect beings—and we in turn create more imperfect people with further flawed experiences. And yet we are expected to be great individuals despite these encounters. Michelle Obama's book *Becoming* is a phenomenal reminder that we are all continually becoming who we are and that we never arrive at a *specific* state of being.[1] I'm grateful for this shortcoming because of the alternative. What if we arrive at a not-so-great state of being? Do we stay there? For how long? The fact that we are constantly becoming gives us a chance to transform what isn't great and to make better whatever is good and then become great and then even greater. That said, every day we are becoming what people and experiences make us.

Our job is to identify what we have become thus far, take responsibility for it, and dedicate ourselves to changing course. I realize that I have become a flawed being and that I have to work each day, each second, to become the person God created me to be and fulfill his purpose for my life. Consciously battling to deny my flesh and submitting to the Spirit to live as a righteous *Man* seem like good ways to start. The things that hurt us, the things that cause us pain, are the things that compel us to make decisions to avoid pain rather than decisions that will honor our purpose.

DRIVEN TO DISTRACTION

Please be clear about this: When we avoid pain, we are serving ourselves. When we honor purpose, we are serving others. If each *Man*'s purpose in life is to be of service, then, put simply, a *Man* is measured by his commitment to service. And since we know each *Man*'s life is to be marked by service, each *Man* should be an agent for healing or restoration.

Grown males do not have or make that kind of commitment. (Have you made the connection yet?) Grown males avoid pain and subsequently serve themselves. They look to be served in order to be distracted from the painful issues that leave them stuck in the difficult spaces of maleness. Our fleshly experiences begin to inform us that we should avoid our issues and pacify our pain with distractions.

How do we recognize distractions? Distractions come in various forms. People often seem happy when they're distracted, but they begin to suffer from the effects of unresolved pain or traumatic events. Distractions cause instability and can significantly increase the risk of mental disorders, substance abuse, sexual promiscuity, and chronic physical ailments, as well as premature death and suicide to name a few.

In contrast, a *Man* deals with his pain to become whole enough to be of service to those around him and thus further matriculate into manhood. When a *Man* is at the peak of his manhood, he will find fulfillment in his purpose of serving others. Secretly, it is the purpose of every living being to help one another, and a *Man* in the most elevated space of manhood will become a model whom others look to mirror.

MISERY LOVES COMPANY

In the last chapter, I introduced my five pain languages with the acronym LUCAS:

Lusting = the passion of pain
Unforgivingness = the memory of pain
Cursing = the vocabulary of pain
Anger = the emotion of pain
Sarcasm = the humor of pain

Much of what we experience in the area of pain comes from these areas. With that said, many of us look to create pain in others so that we have company in our journey of hurt. Misery, or in this case pain, hates to be alone. The sayings "Hurt people hurt people" and "Misery loves company" are very true. The problem is, while we don't necessarily want other people to feel as bad as we do, we were built to be communal,[2] and we usually want company, no matter where we are or what state we're in. Yet when we don't adequately deal with our pain, when we let distractions keep us from dealing with those issues, we put other people in the position of having to deal with our pain instead. Mismanaged pain has a residual effect on others. Humans are naturally programmed to find and create their own tribes. Humans in pain create *tribes* of pain.

Messaging we receive from other people who are themselves hurt, through the scope of LUCAS, is a powerful source that feeds our pain. Messaging we receive from our parents, teachers, friends, and strangers heavily influences who we become. In fact, messaging becomes the launchpad for our trajectory in life. It informs what we become and how we become it. Negative messaging becomes the assassin of a godly life. It literally renders us helpless until we become conscious of its power.

Negative messaging becomes the infomercial of our life, the infomercial we play on a loop in our head every day until we eventually believe it must be true. How many times have you seen a product pitched on a television infomercial and initially said to yourself, *This product is a waste of money because it can't possibly work*? You were skeptical, and you were convinced, based on what you felt in your spirit, that the product was not something you should invest in because of its lack of authenticity. However, you allowed your flesh to make you watch the infomercial, and the longer you watched, despite what you felt in your spirit, the more you began to believe the messaging. Subsequently, you bought into it and merely took its word over your own discernment. You put your good judgment aside and invested in the infomercial enough to buy the product. I know enough about human nature to know I can't be the only one who has made this mistake. But at the same time, mistakes can bring lessons with them.

Negative messaging can work the same way. It becomes the infomercial of a life of unfulfilled purpose: the messaging is that you are the sum of your pain. The product being sold to you is your "SOS"—your "state of stuck." Just as inaccurate as the infomercial on television, the negative messaging about your life becomes the narrative you believe, and it ultimately controls your life's trajectory—forever! Well, until you finish this chapter, that is.

As *Men*, we have to believe the Creator, not the beings who have been created, to determine what we believe we can become. Unfortunately, the acceptance of negative messaging can serve as an opiate for our pain, bringing dire consequences with it.

When I was a kid, I was constantly told I was too skinny, too light to be "really black," too nice to be a boyfriend, and so on. It has been said that it takes a thousand "attaboys" to erase one "you're an idiot." This notion suggests we have to get plenty of positive messaging in order to silence the negative messaging. I have found that the loudest message playing in my head is the one that usually comes true.

When we don't deal with our pain, it deals with us and sinks us into a state of stuck. We might call it the ultimate "sunken place" for a *Man*. I have used "SOS" as a label for our state of stuck because it becomes our cry for help when we don't deal with our pain decisively. Dealing with our pain fortifies us. It is necessary for a healthy life and a positive trajectory.

Trajectory is possibility! The trajectory of our future is not concrete. It is merely the possibility of our outcome if we continue to invest wisely in it. If at any point we decide to deviate from that possibility and invest in another less substantial possibility,

> *When we don't deal with our pain, it deals with us and sinks us into a state of stuck.*

then on that day, our trajectory changes. Pain lies hidden in many places, and if we don't give ourselves emotional checkups, we will be at its mercy until we do.

As previously mentioned, if I had not dealt with the pain that was being peddled in my life, I'm certain I never would have had the courage to write this book. One of the most profound pains that had to be healed was the pain that came in the form of an absent parent.

MY FATHER

My father and I had been estranged from each other for more than two decades when my daughter sat next to me on the couch for a conversation about him. To begin, my father had been incarcerated on a number of occasions throughout my boyhood. One time he had even taken me from my mother and left me in the backseat of his car while he was in the midst of his distractions and caught in the throes of his "maleness." In plain English, he was with a female. No doubt giving in to his flesh. So you can imagine that I had many negative feelings about him when my daughter began to ask me about her nonexistent grandfather.

Our conversation had no segue from any previous discussions. Out of the blue she began to ask me tough questions about my father and why we were no longer connected. Initially, I wanted to lie to her to save myself from the embarrassment of admitting that I hadn't yet dealt with my pain and that I was prideful, holding a grudge and essentially judging my father. Amazingly, I had given grace to every person in my life except my father. Now I was being questioned by one of the very people I was supposed to model good behavior to. She asked me, "Was your dad a good dad to you?" I quickly responded, "He might have been if he wasn't in jail!"

It was an emotional ejaculation. It felt good in the moment because I had jabbed at my father. He had deeply hurt me. But I quickly noticed that I had hurt my daughter in the process. She was now dealing with pain I had caused because of revelations about her grandfather. Additionally, she realized I didn't have the same kind of fatherly experience she had. This caused her even more pain. It was then I had a "coming to Jesus" moment and realized I was teaching her many of the things I never wanted her to do.

Out of my five pain languages, I was teaching her three of them. *Lusting* wasn't one of them because it wasn't a part of the equation of my father and me. I had long since stopped *cursing*, but I was teaching her *unforgivingness* because I had not yet reconciled my feelings about my father, *anger* because I still felt great animosity toward him, and finally *sarcasm* because I had made a bitterly humorous jab at his parental shortfalls. I'm sure this attitude was devastating to her because I was speaking of my very own father, and if I could do this to him, then I was probably capable of doing it to anyone—maybe even her if I thought she had hurt me deeply enough. My father's abandonment hurt me profoundly. Twenty years later, he was still able to activate this bad attitude in me.

I came to realize later that I needed to have empathy for my biological father—not for the nearly seventy-year-old being he was, but for the seven-year-old boy he used to be. I realized his father had probably abandoned him, and thus he couldn't father me because *he* was unfathered. Remember that a male doesn't need to be fathered by his biological father, but he does need to be fathered. (I was first fathered by my stepfather. He took the responsibility of covering me and my mother. That was my first example of manhood at the age of two years old.) The minute I saw my biological father as my "fellow brother" who didn't get what he needed to become a *Man*, my hurt and pain began to dissipate. I apologized to my daughter and assured her that I was going to reconcile with my father. She was wonderfully empathetic and understanding.

Not long after this discussion, I flew back east to witness my goddaughter's high school graduation. Afterward, I decided to drive into Brooklyn to reconcile with my biological father. It didn't take long to realize he had become a *Man* whose standards of behavior were now governed by his faith. He had become similar to the *Man* I had become. While we were of different doctrines and called our God something different, we were, nonetheless, *Men* of faith. He was humble and contrite, and soon I had a new level of respect and empathy for him.

I recognized that he could have become a great *Man* if he had received what so many of us are missing: stable parental training, which is so vital for children during their developmental years. Nonetheless, he had received spiritual guidance while in prison through Islam. Therefore, as his "fellow brother," I was proud of his matriculation into manhood. As his son, I was elated for the *Man* from whom I had gotten half of my DNA.

MY SON

Hurt and pain come throughout our lives and usually affect us until we become aware of them and someone helps us address these companions. But there are times when we are too young to even realize that our hearts and spirits have become infected with the virus of pain. For this reason, it is essential that our caretakers are conscious of their duty to help us become and remain as whole as possible so that we don't unknowingly turn into adults who fall victim to LUCAS. Without such a safeguard, many of us sustain emotional and mental injuries that go unaddressed and cause powerful infections to the head and heart. These doses of pain become the assailant that attacks our health and wholeness, thus robbing the world of countless would-be men of enormous worth.

This thought brings me to my son. At the age of nine, he encountered a kid—a friend at school we'll call Ben—who called him a racial epithet. Now, for most human beings, name-calling is a source of profound hurt, but for a

Hurt and pain come throughout our lives and usually affect us until we become aware of them and someone helps us address these companions.

child with no coping and recognition skills, it can be utterly confusing and set him or her on a harmful trajectory. I immediately began triage on my son's spirit by asking him how he felt. While in tears, he admitted he was hurt because he considered Ben to be a pretty good friend. It's the kind of position no parent ever wants to be put in.

My son Dré was in great pain, and I knew we had to deal with the hurt and disappointment immediately. If we didn't, his pain would deal with him later in life. Imagine being shot by a small-caliber bullet and deciding to let it stay inside you because you don't want to deal with the pain of removing it. The real pain is the pain that comes with not dealing with the issue, which will become even greater as long as it goes unaddressed.

My son and I had a powerful conversation about how kids

regurgitate things they hear while not understanding the full impact of what they are saying and to whom they are saying it. He seemed to get it and was quickly feeling relief from his pain as he gained clarity from his confusion. As his father, I was dealing with my own pain—the pain of feeling helpless because another person had caused my son to become less whole. It hurt even further since I had coached Ben on my son's baseball team. Therefore, I spoke with all parties involved—Ben's mom, who actually alerted me about the situation before I even heard it from the school (which was a problem), Ben himself, and, of course, the school's administration.

The conversation I had with Ben's mom proved to be quite productive, despite the sensitive nature of the subject. To her credit, the mom couldn't have been more apologetic. She vowed to have Ben deal directly with me because she wanted him to come to an understanding about race from a black *Man* and hoped this approach would give Ben proper perspective, along with care and consideration. Her trust in me to handle Ben, who had dealt my son such a devastating blow, was a great indication of what she thought of me, of how much she respected and trusted me as a *Man*.

I had a transformative conversation with Ben, along with my son and the dean of the school, who is also a great advocate of mine. That meeting left both boys feeling clear about what had happened and why it had happened. Physically, children are pliable, but mentally and emotionally, they can be only as pliable as their understanding allows them to be. Once they have been adequately instructed and informed, they can recover rather quickly. But left to their own devices, they can easily become predatory.

I then had a conversation with their teacher, who had chosen not to call me about the incident. Our exchange was initially an awkward one because I truly felt that if the mom hadn't informed me about the incident, I might never have learned about it. This is how children are left at a deficit in life. They will become something outside of what we teach them when we are uninformed about their emotional and mental injuries.

Deciding not to apprise me of this incident was both unwise and uninformed on the part of the boys' teacher. It showed that even teachers have their blind spots. Again, we are all human and capable of making decisions that can cause great pain. If my son and Ben's mother had also kept this incident from me, these boys might have chosen a destructive path, suddenly or eventually. Ben's mother and I wouldn't have known when this disturbing route was first taken, why it was considered, or how to help redirect the boys.

I pointed out to their teacher that if my son were to sustain a physical injury on her watch, she would call the nurse to address his wounds so that the wounds wouldn't get infected and cause harm to the body. After caring for the wound, the nurse would send home a notice of his physical injury so that we could follow up with proper care of that wound at home. Taking this measure would help ensure that the physical wound healed properly and that the body had a chance to regain its health and wholeness. But how does an emotional and mental injury, like being called a racial epithet, heal when no one addresses it and the child is left to fend for himself or herself? It will likely become infected and produce a profoundly hurt person who may turn into an angry adult as a result of neglect.

Anger, simply put, is profound hurt. In most instances, anger shows up to help ensure that the affected individual doesn't get hurt anymore. Therefore, I had to impress upon the teacher that I had to nurse the emotional and mental injuries of my son and that

I must be made aware of emotional injuries, just as with physical ones, so those wounds can be addressed properly to avoid any spiritual infection. Otherwise, my son and others like him might become a part of the statistical group of males whose development gets arrested. They never mature into manhood.

The teacher's actions were not nefarious, just unconscious. But they could have brought on irreversible consequences. Eventually, she realized the severity of such consequences and the potential damage to children. Having gained clarity from our conversation, she understood my requirements and agreed to meet them should the need arise in the future.

I kept calm throughout our conversation. I didn't yell or curse at her, which would have caused her the kind of pain I was feeling. I avoided all of that despite the fact that my flesh was trying to give me permission to. As *Men*, we must remain calm in the midst of chaos, no matter how hurt and eventually angry we may become. However, where loved ones are concerned, this admonition is far easier said than done.

Then an idea struck in the midst of the calm. Through all of my son's pain and even my own, I decided to do something that had gone unmodeled for me in the streets of Brooklyn but was modeled for me by Christ, the embodiment of God in the flesh. Christ is the model I decided to mirror rather than allow my anger to inform my actions in moving forward. I chose to do something transformative. I chose to be a servant by creating an assembly for all of the grades in my son's school to talk about the power of words and their ability to inflict hurt and pain on those around us.

If my son had been a victim of someone's words, then someone else's child may have been as well. Maybe, without me even knowing it, my son had unconsciously done something similar to someone else's child. For this reason, I tried to create a restorative moment out of a devastative one.

I gave what essentially became a TED Talk for the kids. I told them to ask themselves, *Before I do what I'm about to do or say what I'm about to say, what are my intentions?* Next I asked them to use language and actions that would *cultivate* someone's spirit, not *crush* their spirit. I encouraged them to be kind and not callous. I reminded them that our lapses in kindness portray us as callous and promote the very things that deposit huge amounts of hurt into the lives of the people we encounter.

Knowing how they would hate homework, I gave them a social experiment to conduct. I asked them to do something or say something to another child they didn't know and then note how their actions or words changed that child's countenance afterward. I gave this talk to prekindergartners through sixth graders. This mission took most of my day, but I think about what it did for each of those kids and what it may have done, I hope, for countless other people. By submitting to God's call on my life as a servant, I hoped to create other mindful young servants. I can only pray my mission was successful.

Giving this talk helped me address the hurt I was experiencing and further helped my son address his. I also modeled something I hope he'll remember for the rest of his life. Lastly, I wanted to deal with Ben's pain as well, a blind spot for him as it is for most nine-year-olds. I wanted to pour something into him that would have a huge personal impact, something from a black *Man* to a white child. This endeavor was a pretty big deal for both of us, as well as for the rest of the students. Our society is racially charged, and we all need to receive messaging from a myriad of people from diverse backgrounds.

LOOKING LIKE YOUR DADDY

A *Man*'s job is to take care of the children and women in his life, not just his own or the ones who make him proud, but *all* children and *all* women, and to do so with thoughtful consideration. To love others and *demonstrate* this love is what separates every *Man* from his grown male counterparts. The mark of a *Man* is that he *can* lead with his physicality but *chooses* to lead with his mentality. As the saying goes, "You were born looking like your Daddy [God], but you will die looking like your decisions!"

The mark of a Man *is that he* can *lead with his physicality but* chooses *to lead with his mentality.*

A *Man* has to realize that every decision made in his life affects not only him but all those around him too. He has to think of himself as the navigation system of his house and community. His decisions will either spark life or summon death by hurting someone's spirit. A *Man* should lead his tribe in ways that effectively deal with their pain. If a *Man* denies his pain, his pain will deal with him by leaving him in the "SOS" of life. If he effectively deals with his pain, he begins to heal himself and subsequently models for those around him an admirable way to live life. You cannot heal if you do not deal!

CHAPTER 5

AUTHENTICITY, CLARITY, AND EMPATHY

I trust you are enjoying our journey thus far. Our next adventure lands us in a place that is familiar to many of us—church. I have often been asked when I'm going to open my own church, and I usually ask those folks why they would like to see me serve in that capacity. Most of them reply the same way: "Because you make things relatable and give life context through realistic scenarios. And you often use the Scriptures to do so." While I would not consider myself qualified to lead a church and teach a congregation about Scripture, much of how I do what I do comes from the teachings of the Bible.

An example has to do with how we connect with our LGBTQ cousins. I believe we have a generation of young people who have not made a connection to the church. These brothers and sisters have often been so hurt by religion that they have turned away from the church and have subsequently shunned God.

God and church are two separate entities. Some leaders in the church have not found a way to bridge the gap between the LGBTQ community and those in the congregation. As a result, many have *not* found their place in God's story. So while I have no plans to open the doors of a physical church building, I do have a specific purpose in mind for my work: to let the LGBTQ community know that God's love and the love of the truly righteous will not forsake them. When I speak my message, it often sounds like a sermon. So really, to a certain extent, I am doing my brand of church every time I speak. And today is no different. I am going to give you a little bit of church in this chapter.

DEALING WITH OUR ACES

Brothers and sisters (now you know every good sermon usually starts off that way), I would like to deal with how we got to where we are and how to get to where we would like to be. We have avoided God's Word and his assignment for our lives. But now we have to be diligent about uncovering the truth in order to be in proper spiritual alignment.

To do that, I want to talk about the word *ace*. In many things, the *ace* is the optimal point. We want to ace the test. The go-to—the best pitcher on a baseball team—is called the ace. The best shot you can hit in golf is a hole in one, and golfers refer to that as an ace. The highest-ranking card in the deck is the ace of spades. When someone compliments you, he or she says, "That guy is aces!" When you make a serve that cannot be returned, you have served an ace. When someone has something extra special that he or she hasn't revealed to anyone, the person says, "I've got an ace up my sleeve!"

The very definition of the word *ace* is "to perform extremely well in something"—especially in an exam or other high-pressure endeavor. *Ace* refers to something really good, if not the best. Whatever it refers to cannot get any better. However, I'm going to talk about another type of "ace"—one that is not good for any of us.

The acronym ACE stands for "adverse childhood experiences." Many of us suffer great traumas as we grow up, and those traumas act as levers that will shift our trajectories in a way that keeps us operating from a deficit. I distinctly remember becoming aware of my own traumas and how they impacted me when I was introduced to my ACEs. I took an ACE online quiz, which you can find in a web search.[1] I couldn't believe the number of traumas in my boyhood that were strongly affecting my manhood. Childhood trauma is something many of us think we can get away from, but we are truly misled if we think that way.

In this life, whatever we avoid dealing with will assuredly deal with us! It is well documented in studies and quite evidenced in our own lives.[2] Unfortunately, many of us deny what we know to be true. In the short term, denying an adverse experience that has occurred is easier than dealing with the work that must be done in the long term to reconcile the experience. Until we have the courage to deal with the ACEs that informed our boyhood, we will never be able to unlock what I have deemed the ACEs of manhood.

THE ACES OF MANHOOD

The ACEs of manhood are:

Authenticity
Clarity
Empathy

These traits are essential in allowing us to be the *Men* whom God intended us to be when we were created. Without **A**uthenticity, we will be unable to tell the truth to ourselves and be truthful with others, which will certainly lead to a lack of trust. Without **C**larity, we will be unable to make good decisions for ourselves and ultimately be unable to lead others righteously. Without **E**mpathy, we will harbor profound hurt, which usually turns to great anger that keeps us from being able to forgive.

Right now, I want to break down why every male needs each of these three key ingredients for manhood and how each elevates *Men* who are already living it out. We will also discuss biblical examples of godly *Men* and be reminded that there is something higher than ourselves. It is vital to realize we are not God but that we have been made in his image and should live lives that honor our Creator. And one of the greatest ways to live a life that honors God and mirrors the life that Christ modeled for us is to live a life of authenticity, clarity, and empathy.

Before we jump into Scripture, I want to take a minute to explain why this message is so vital for all brothers and sisters, but especially our *brothers*. I once saw an episode of *Law and Order* in which a young boy was repeatedly tortured by his own father because his father was attempting to use the abuse to "make him become a *Man*." We must understand that abuse is not the same thing as discipline. Many of us were not "spanked"; we were beaten. Now, this type of physical treatment is a controversial topic because many of us have been conditioned to believe that abuse and discipline are the same thing, but truly they are not.

That said, as a result of the abuse of the father, the son in this episode decided once and for all to prove to his father that he was a "*Man*." Typical of many males who have a misconception about what manhood is, the son chose to let his aggression lead the way. He gained access to his father's rifles and shot up his school. Fortunately, the boy was eventually disarmed and taken into custody. Interestingly, the district attorney wanted the father to be brought before the court also, where he could be held accountable for the sins of the son.

While the show is fiction, this father is a far too common example of what happens to many sons who are raised in this manner. The sons end up being raised in the ways of their fathers, who are grown males wearing the uniform of a *Man* but are far from actually being one. They are incapable of teaching something they have never been taught. Consequently, the boys go completely unfathered. Although there is a male figure in the house, both father and son go unfathered because of a lack of manhood accountability and messaging. Being unfathered is a dangerous proposition for any male, but even more so for the society that will eventually have to deal with him.

Think about this. The Bible says, "Train up a child in the way he should go; even when he is old he will not depart from it."[3] What does this admonition mean?

We need to give our boys the blueprint for their manhood as we raise them. If a boy is raised by a father who is only a grown male, or if his upbringing is devoid of a father's presence, he is set up to be a problem waiting to happen. Even though *nature* dictates many outcomes in a boy's life, *nurture* has the unique ability to change his trajectory. When no one has nurtured a boy or given him the proper life lessons, what is the boy to do? What does he do when no one has trained him?

A great documentary was released in 2018 called *Three Identical Strangers*. It's about a set of triplets who were separated at birth and adopted by three different families. After they became adults, they found each other and realized they had some eerie similarities. They liked the same type of women, smoked the same brand of cigarettes, folded their legs the same way, spoke in the same patterns, finished each other's sentences, and so on and so on.

These things seemed to tie them together, but many other things had affected the trajectory of their lives. Their DNA, or their "nature," constructed some binding behaviors—like crossing their legs the same way—but their environments and the way they were raised, or their "nurture," was the key factor in setting their individual trajectories and in determining who they would ultimately become.

Unfortunately, the triplets never had anyone help them assess who they were, either as grown males or as *Men*, and they were never afforded the opportunity to correct their course. One of the most profound takeaways was that the film seemed to suggest that the dynamics of a father and his type of presence in the home affect a boy's upbringing more than anything else.

In the documentary, David had an adopted dad who was emotionally unavailable, and subsequently you could see David's tendency to mirror that. Bobby, in contrast, had an adopted dad who was jovial, loving, and warm, and of course this had the same effect on Bobby. Moreover, the film indicated that Eddy had a lot of conflicts with his adopted dad. They had many troubled encounters, and unfortunately, Eddy later committed suicide. While his dad may not be to blame for Eddy's suicide, there is obvious evidence that the part a father or dad figure plays in a boy's life is linked to his future behavioral patterns.

This is the tale of many males all over this country and, of course, all over the world. We should begin to acquire the language required to properly identify ourselves either as grown males or as *Men*. And once we do so, if we finally realize we are merely grown males, we must begin to seek out the kind of *Men* who will help us matriculate into manhood.

THE EXAMPLE OF MOSES— AUTHENTICITY

This is where our Bible All-Stars come in. They represent transformative truths for us today.

Let's start with Moses. He is an exceptional example of authenticity. Here's the Cliffs Notes version of the early life of Moses. You can read the entire account in Exodus 2. But if you go back a chapter to Exodus 1, you will find out that an evil pharaoh was in control. He would eventually try to destroy the Hebrew people altogether, but first he enslaved them. He further decided that he wanted all of the male Hebrew babies to be killed, for he feared they were beginning to outnumber the Egyptians and would eventually pose a threat to them.

When a group of people fail to submit to a higher calling, when they give in to their fears and anxieties, they become a detriment to themselves and everyone around them. They will even go as far as planning the demise of other people to ensure that they remain the dominant group. This mentality makes people paranoid, especially if they discover that their birth rates are down while other populations keep growing. That narrative is eerily similar to the conditions that society is now experiencing, don't you think? The Bible quite often gives us a peek into what we face today, despite the countless years between then and now. You get the point? Amen.

But the Egyptian midwives feared God more than they feared Pharaoh. Instead of killing the male babies, as they had been told to do, they decided to tell Pharaoh that the Hebrew women were delivering babies much faster than the Egyptian women. And because of the speed at which Hebrew women were giving birth, the midwives were unable to fulfill Pharaoh's request. The midwives clearly added to the account, saying that the Hebrew women often had already given birth by the time the Hebrew midwives arrived. Not to be defeated in his purpose, Pharaoh ordered all the infant Hebrew boys to be thrown into the Nile River, but as any powerful grown male would do, he allowed the girls to live in order to serve his own needs.

Around this time, Moses's mother gave birth to him and was able to hide him for three months. When she was no longer able to hide Moses, she put him in a papyrus basket and set it among the reeds of the river. Moses's sister, carefully and from afar, followed the basket down the river and watched as Pharaoh's daughter found the basket and decided to keep Moses. (I know many of you are familiar with this story, but I am going somewhere with this.)

Fast-forward to years later, when Moses is a young man who has been raised in the enemy's house. Moses has learned Pharaoh's language, consumed his food, and been taught the practices and customs of the Egyptians. It would have been easy for Moses to keep living the good life in the palace while his people were suffering, but he just couldn't be silent. He could not stand by and watch while his people were being mistreated.

If you have children, you may have seen *The Prince of Egypt*, the animated musical motion picture released by DreamWorks in 1998. If you haven't seen it, I highly recommend it. The event that set Moses up for his first transformative step as a *Man* was when Moses killed an Egyptian taskmaster who had whipped a Hebrew for not working hard enough. Now, while we shouldn't condone violence, we cannot be men who stand by while our people, especially our women, children, and elderly, are mistreated. We must take a stand against the cowards who attempt to bully our people into ungodly submission of any kind.

Meanwhile, back in Moses's world, Moses embraced the first step in his journey to manhood: *authenticity.* We witness two dosages of authenticity during this whole ordeal. The midwives set the tone for it by disobeying an order that seemed to go against their very purpose in life. For a midwife in charge of bringing life into the world, the command to snuff out a life brings one face-to-face with one's authenticity or lack of it. Now, if the midwives set the tone for authenticity, then Moses hammered it home! Moses could no longer sit comfortably in the house of Pharaoh while his people were being mistreated. He could have basked in the comfort of Pharaoh's house and allowed his flesh to be fed for as long as he wished. But he denied his flesh and stood on his faith to become the servant God intended him to be. The story of the *Man* who would eventually lead his people into the Red Sea and watch God perform the miracle of peeling back the waters so the Hebrew people could walk across on dry land started with a young man who decided to take Robert Frost's "the road less traveled" and stand up for freedom.

An important step to achieving manhood is being authentic. Those who are called to be leaders will never reach their full potential or activate their purpose until they decide to live as an original masterpiece handcrafted by God instead of an imitation, a knockoff, trying to be someone else. Holding fast to self-determination is one of the blessings of deciding to be *you*—even when you mess up and go too far. Remember that while Moses stopped the beating of his fellow countryman (a true brother), he killed another "brother" in the process.

An important step to achieving manhood is being authentic.

As was the case with Moses, God is still able to take our mess and turn it into a message. He is able to turn our test into a testimony, and he is able to use our life to save someone else's, all in the name of *service*—the true mark of a *Man*.

As I've suggested, Moses was not perfect. He struck the rock when God had clearly given him a specific directive to speak to the rock.[4] Also, as previously mentioned, Moses killed an Egyptian overseer[5]—which leads to the point that Moses's disobedience kept him from going into the promised land.[6] For as humble a servant as Moses was, this admirable trait did not make him exempt from accountability to God.

Herein lies a lesson for all of us: *Do not allow people, places, or platforms to serve as the reason you miss your blessing!* Be authentically righteous. God will always use you, but there are some opportunities you will not get again if you allow your emotions to make you act out of character or let peer pressure predict your predicament. In other words, don't allow others to alter your decision making. We have to access our authenticity by fully understanding and acknowledging our true identity.

THE EXAMPLE OF SAUL/PAUL—CLARITY

Having dealt with authenticity, we now need to address *clarity*. One of the *Men* who displays great clarity in the Bible is the apostle Paul. Let us begin with the fact that he started his journey in history as one who brought chaos to the church. This brother hated Christians and harassed and persecuted the followers of Christ. As the Spirit was at work on the road to Damascus, Paul had an encounter with the true and living God. It was reported that Paul, then named Saul, was blinded![7] Now my personal feeling is that at crucial times in life, we are all blind to the truth. *We lack clarity.* It was quite apparent that Saul couldn't see the truth about Christ, the truth that God is the Most High and the powerful Creator. Saul constantly went out of his way to persecute Christians. In fact, it was as if this Pharisee's mission was to be an enemy of God and Christianity.

We could argue that Saul was blind even while having his physical sight. He couldn't see the truth about Christ or God and certainly couldn't see himself as "a servant of Christ Jesus, called to be an apostle."[8] He had no clarity, so in turn he was blind to the truth, and it completely affected his trajectory as a *Man*. When he was finally "blinded" by the light of Christ, I believe that Saul was forced, maybe for the first time in his life, to truly submit. As I said before, one of the keys to a *Man*'s growth and matriculation into manhood is the acknowledgment of something higher than himself. The minute we think we are the highest, we begin to feel the expectation that other people must serve us. But the minute we realize there is something higher than us, we see that we were intended to be humble servants.

Do you think Saul was humbled when he lost his sight? Do you think his loss of sight and his newfound humility made him open to being the servant he was intended to be? Certainly! Now, do not be confused. Just because you don't have sight does not mean you lack vision. Ray Charles did not have sight, but he had vision. Stevie Wonder does not have sight, but he has vision. Louis Braille did not have sight, but he had vision.

I believe God took away Saul's *physical* sight and killed his flesh in order to make way for his *spiritual* vision, which served to birth his faith. God could have gotten his attention in myriad ways, but I know it is not coincidental that God would take his sight and then restore it, because sometimes God needs us to see what *he* sees. God needs us to see what he sees *for our lives.*

God needed Saul to have clarity and to see himself as Paul the apostle, who would go on to write a good portion of the New Testament, plant churches, and teach the gospel. God needs us to gain clarity so that we can take up a mission of sacrifice and service to help males become *Men.* God needs *Men* to have vision—the kind of vision that will allow us to walk in sustained clarity so that our children can grow up in homes with fathers. God needs men to walk in clarity so that we can help our incarcerated brothers break free of the chains that put them behind bars so that when they get out, they will never go back. *Clarity* is an essential theme of the everyday life of the *Man* we are intended to be so that every generation can be better, stronger, and wiser. And since we are having church right now, go ahead and say, "Amen!"

Clarity *is an essential theme of the everyday life of the* Man *we are intended to be so that every generation can be better, stronger, and wiser.*

THE EXAMPLE OF JESUS—EMPATHY

Once a *Man* is authentic and has clarity, he is prepared to address empathy! *Empathy* has become a new twenty-first-century buzzword that seems to have supplanted the word *sympathy* as the go-to notion for fully feeling human beings. *Sympathy* has come to mean you have compassion, sorrow, or pity for someone's misfortune or hardship. *Empathy* goes deeper into the human connection, and we generally do not go through life well without empathy. In author Daniel Pink's book *A Whole New Mind*, he brilliantly defines *empathy* this way: "Empathy is the ability to imagine yourself in someone else's position and to intuit what that person is feeling. It is the ability to stand in others' shoes, to see with their eyes, and to feel with their hearts."[9] This word has been around only since the mid-1800s and is not used in the King James Bible. Nonetheless, there are Bible passages that show us what empathy looks like.

Paul the apostle urged Christ's followers to "rejoice with those who rejoice; mourn with those who mourn."[10] This is clearly an expression of empathy, and by sharing in other people's emotions, we are able to live life as a close-knit and godly family. The apostle Peter urged us to be empathetic to others by being "like-minded" and having a "tender heart."[11] Both Paul and Peter clearly urge that we be at one with our brothers and sisters and go deeper to be more spiritual than the average person, who may simply settle for being sympathetic. Empathy is vital to us as *Men* because it is usually a catalyst for action. It propels us into a space that allows us to be God's conduit for all things righteous.

Our Savior, Jesus, truly is the greatest example of an empathetic *Man*—with all due respect to Joseph, the favored son of Jacob. For all that Joseph did for his brothers, choosing not to treat them in ways their sins caused them to deserve, he gets an honorable mention. Christ, however, is the total embodiment of empathy. The Gospels are replete with instances in which Jesus showed himself as a *Man* of empathy.

And it was Jesus' willingness to take on human flesh that showed the very essence of his empathy. This empathy he did not hoard like a pitiable miser; he shared it repeatedly as a giving Savior. He empathized with the fearful, the depressed, the alienated, the convicted, the conflicted, the afflicted, the lost, the least, and the last. And, amazingly, Jesus dealt with each of these in his own way and on their individual level.

The greatest gift of empathy is Christ's giving up his life for all of our sins. He so empathized with our struggle on this earth, the one that stems from our flesh, that he literally gave his own flesh as a sacrifice so that we might come to know God. The ultimate servant, who never failed to be empathetic, gave us the most profound example of empathy and showed how we must be committed to honoring his example. Each time I think about his thoughtfulness and his sacrifice, I'm able to remain in a space of empathy. The key is reminding myself of that thoughtfulness and sacrifice.

The ability to show empathy is essential to our manhood; it is the sine qua non—the thing that is *absolutely essential*! When *Men* are showing empathy, we are saying, without using words, that we have heard the pleas of our brothers or sisters, and we are at our best when we answer and fulfill this "Macedonian call."[12]

Men of empathy become more loving, gentle, calm, amenable, genuine, and serving.

Furthermore, *Men* of empathy become more loving, gentle, calm, amenable, genuine, and serving. We often run from being empathetic because we feel less than manly when we share the suffering of a brother or sister in the household of faith. However, I agree with whoever said, "No man stands taller than when he kneels to help another."

Jesus serves as the bridge between God and us. He is the perfect model of one who embraces two natures—the nature of God and the fleshly nature of a human being. At the same time, his example shows that we are privileged to participate in these two natures—that we can embrace our godly nature and fight against the desires of our human nature, especially selfishness.

In short, Jesus was concerned about *pleasing* God and had total disregard for *impressing* man. Likewise, people who come into your presence should soon be able to discern what you are all about. I am not suggesting that you or any other person can be perfect, for the Bible provides abundant examples of individuals who were not. Samson was not good at determining in whom to confide; Peter disowned our Lord, though he loved Jesus with all his heart. We all make mistakes in the pursuit of perfection, but we should never faint while we are pursuing it. Seeking to become more empathetic daily is a good starting point.

To me, one of Christ's most valuable teachings is that I need to have empathy for myself as well. I grew up in an undesirable environment in the city of Brooklyn, and frequently it was unforgiving. As a result of spending many years navigating Brooklyn's streets, I learned *unforgivingness*. I remind myself daily that while I arrived on this earth with the potential to honor God and to do what pleases him, my life experiences have derailed me from his intention for my life. And many years later, I slowly learned that empathy is the route to restoration and service.

These three ingredients make a life dedicated to reaching manhood doable, sustainable, and durable. Life with demonstrated empathy will be honorable, while life without it will be hollow. Remember, you are not your ACEs (adverse childhood experiences), but your manhood should always exemplify your ACEs (authenticity, clarity, and empathy).

Let the church say, "Amen!"

CHAPTER 6

YOU FIRST:

Defining Servant Leadership

Back on the campus of *Man* U, we are having a fireside chat with the brothers about the importance of "being first." To many people, this will seem counterintuitive. For those who have been taught that women and children come first, this fireside chat will seem rude and ungentlemanly. Women and children do come first as it relates to our major priorities in life, but I'm talking about "being first" in terms of being the first to do something that *serves as a model* for other people. *Men* should constantly strive to serve and lead by example—*first*!

> Men *should constantly strive to serve and lead by example—first!*

How often have you heard people say, "You first"? They'll often say, "I'll do what you do *after* you do it first." It happens all the time. We live in a culture in which people expect to be *served* rather than to be of *service*. We open the door for ourselves without holding it for others or get something to eat without asking others if they're hungry. While these examples may be basic, they speak to deeper issues.

We also live in a time when there are far more sheep than shepherds. More people will be inclined to follow rather than lead. In fact, the easiest way to get people to do something is to do it first because people are usually inclined to mimic behavior. Very rarely do people do what you *tell* them to do. This world has become a place where people see or hear about behaviors and follow their lead—from something as meaningless as fashion trends to something as serious as copycat crimes. Therefore we should constantly be doing things we want other people to do.

As *Men*, we have to take our rightful place as the leaders we were intended to be. Now, of course, this admonition does not mean that women are incapable of being leaders or that they should not be leaders. What it does mean is that grown males have been damaging the brand of *Man* for far too long by living like boys without the mental and emotional capacity to matriculate into manhood—which should be the true definition of "growing up."

Generally speaking, because *Men*—not males—don't normally make decisions from an emotional place first, we often can make great leaders. However, our cross to bear is that we can sometimes make decisions that call attention to our physicality first—decisions that can be dangerous for us and those around us. As *Men*, we have to demonstrate that we are true leaders, not by *telling* people what to do, but by *showing* them what to do.

Imagine a typical pool party. How many times have you been invited to a pool party and not one person is in the pool? Now, don't get me wrong; most of the time, all who are present are enjoying themselves—the music, the food, and the conversation—but no one is enjoying the very essence of the party. This happens quite often, in fact. People will use something as a device to gather people but will seldom be engaged in the actual device.

Whenever I have the opportunity, even with something as unimportant as a pool party, I make it a point to get into the water in order to spur others' participation as well. Being first. Modeling behavior that I want to have mirrored is a practice. It is in the spirit of "follow the leader," which allows me to get better at whatever I endeavor to do. You would be shocked at how many people mimic behavior after it is demonstrated, particularly if it is done with precision and consistency. Few things in life happen until someone goes first.

Something similar happens on Sundays. The device for church on Sunday is the Bible, but few people will engage in it. Likewise, the device for males to elevate themselves in life is manhood, but few will engage in it. The way to attract people to engage in something is to allow them to witness *us* engaging it first, demonstrating that it's not only safe but also good for us.

BE FIRST FOR YOUR KIDS

I am on a mission to encourage, motivate, and empower *Men* to step up, to "be first," to be models of service to others. Even my ten-year-old son has noticed.

One day while I was writing in the family room, my son was studying for one of his weekly spelling and vocabulary tests in the breakfast nook with my wife. They were behind me so I couldn't see them, but I could hear them clearly. While studying with him, my wife and I will typically have him spell the word, define it, and then use it in a sentence. After a series of words, they came upon the word *impact*. He spelled the word with relative ease and defined it just as easily. My wife then asked him to use it in a sentence, and without hesitation he said, "My daddy makes an *impact* on people!"

You can well imagine what an emotion-packed time that was for me. I heard my son acknowledging my level of service, indicating that not only had he benefited from my messaging, but he observed that others had too. Children cannot be fooled into saying something they really do not connect with. Very rarely do they lie about their impressions because they are unafraid of the unbridled truth. So they typically don't tend to lie.

Lying is a skill—not a good one, obviously—and like most skills, it becomes a learned behavior that takes practice. Repetition in acquiring and applying any new skill or skill set is essential. Contrary to popular opinion, most behaviors are not innate in humans. Racism, sexism, xenophobia, misogyny, and any other biases are learned behaviors. People must have them repeated before they reprogram their spirit. I digress, but I had to drive home the point that behaviors, like "being first," are learned and require repetition in order to become part of the self. You're going to have to *practice* serving others.

EXAMPLES OF BEING FIRST IN THE BIBLE

Believers have the most powerful example of "being first" ever demonstrated. Just as we concluded in our last chapter, Jesus Christ serves as the model we all can mirror. He went first and redeemed all humankind. Christ died first, knowing that some people would never appreciate his sacrifice or even take advantage of the benefit of it. It is the perfect template for manhood.

There is actually a protective blessing that occurs in the spiritual and the natural when men take their rightful places in their families and in their communities. When Paul the apostle says in Ephesians 5:23 that "the husband is the head of the wife" and makes his point clear by saying "as Christ is the head of the church," he's drawing up the blueprint for manhood. And then in verse 25 he drives it home further by saying that husbands should love their wives "just as Christ loved the church and gave himself up for her" to make it perfectly clear that a *Man*'s assignment in life is to love women and children like Christ loved—as a sacrificial servant leader who puts the needs of all others ahead of his own. He was setting the tone for *Men* to be first in his service.

As I consider the pressure and the struggles we *Men* face, I often think of Adam and imagine how different life might have been had Adam just called out to God and admitted that although his helpmate, his wife, had given him the fruit, they both had eaten from the tree. Instead, Adam blamed Eve, who in turn blamed the serpent.

Adam's version of "being first" was a bad one. Adam lied first and disastrously modeled for Eve what she ultimately mirrored. When he deliberately lied, not taking responsibility for his actions, his wife quickly followed his example. Modeling works far more than we give it credit for, and sadly it worked in this instance as well. In many relationships, modeling turns into a crazy blame cycle that keeps all involved spinning as if they were on the hamster wheel of life.

Yes, it is much easier to act out of our flesh and blame others than to take the courageous step of responsibility. But again, through habitual practice, we must reach the point where it feels better to take responsibility than to bear the weight of lying and self-deception and not holding oneself accountable. Unfortunately, we see lack of accountability in many areas of life. The category of males who lack manhood is probably the most powerful example. It is the reason we have the Me Too and Time's Up movements. Grown males have singlehandedly given these movements rocket fuel. And for good reason. Grown males who do not strive to develop their manhood are doing great damage by swelling these ranks. Those males who hold positions of power and lack self-control provide confusing examples as to whether they are grown males or *Men*. Again, simply *looking* like *Men* physically does not make them *Men* mentally, emotionally, and spiritually. Woefully, a lack of self-control has been the *unmaking* of hordes of self-made grown males!

The immigration crisis in America has been crying out for *Men* who will speak out against this shameful dilemma, no matter what their partisan position may be. Decent human beings, particularly those who try to live righteously by the Spirit, cannot in good conscience justify the neglect and mistreatment of people, especially children, who find themselves alone in a strange land and separated from their parents. Nothing is more painful to me than watching grown males not "being first" in protest and peaceful activism against the deplorable practices of our nation. Labeling immigrants as subhuman, separating families, and allowing the abuse of children should never be tolerated.

We were designed in the image of God, so being protectors is infused into our very DNA. We need to see ourselves as the trees that we are. Without the cover of a tree, many of us would burn from the harmful heat coming from a self-serving source that is on fire with greed and uncaring. A *Man* and his assignment are very much like a real tree. When a *Man* fails to cover the women and children in his life by "being first," he carelessly exposes them to people who are being consumed by the harmful elements of this world. The Bible says in Psalm 92:12–15:

> The righteous will flourish like a palm tree,
> they will grow like a cedar of Lebanon;

planted in the house of the LORD,

they will flourish in the courts of our God.

They will still bear fruit in old age,

they will stay fresh and green,

proclaiming, "The LORD is upright;

he is my Rock, and there is no wickedness in him."

Men, moreover, have been ordained to protect the powerless by stepping out, speaking out, and taking charge, even when it is unpopular. In fact, when the cause is not popular, it is usually a signal that we must move steadfastly into action. So, my brothers, from now on, see yourself as the tree that provides cover for all those around you. And do it *first*!

ACTING LIKE A *MAN*

I portrayed a character on a television show that was created to tell a story about my people. Because it was done with great precision and accuracy, it had a profound effect on people who watched it, particularly people of color. Almost daily, women would approach me to tell me what a tremendous impact my character had on them and how it gave them hope that there was a *Man* somewhere in the world like that for them.

I felt their pain deeply as a *Man* who watched some of the women in my life struggle with relationships where manhood was not present. Each woman I talked to, because I could see the pain, became a sister I wanted to protect and for whom I wanted to provide the kind of *Man* they richly deserved. If I couldn't play matchmaker for them in real life, I wanted to give them a peek at what a *Man* really is and how he covers them and his community. I wanted to honor each of them, as I would my grandmother (may she rest in peace), my mother, my wife, and my daughter. This character had come to represent on television something that rarely gets represented regarding our community—that *Men* do exist.

Now, as I have stated frequently in this book, a grown male is a male who generally looks to be served, while a *Man* is a male who generally looks to be of service. The character I was playing represented so much to our viewership. He was a model of service and a pillar of his community—a professor at a prestigious university who exhibited honor, uprightness, and integrity. But the character was about to take a drastic turn.

The new scripts called for him to suddenly break up with his girlfriend, stop serving his community—mostly because of the breakup—begin dating his ex-girlfriend's sister, and start smoking marijuana. This drastic change felt like the death of a vision and a reversal of hope for all of those women I had encountered. If this character were white, he would have been called "McDreamy." But instead he was quickly turned into "McDreary." It felt as though I was perpetuating negative myths about *Men*—in particular, black men (not males, but *Men*)—that *Men* navigate dating choices solely based on physical needs, and that they will abandon their duty to their community when they don't get what they want. And of course the popular lie that all black men smoke weed.

I knew we would be cementing the theory that we are all the same. That there is no delineation between being a *Man* and being a grown male. While I respected the fact that the show had the right to tell that story, as a *Man*—and again, as a black man whom society already labeled as dangerous and irresponsible—I knew I couldn't tell that story with truthful precision. Why? Because it is a lie. And since I did not like the story that was being told about *Men*, I knew I had to further dedicate myself to teaching males how to become *Men* so the stories about them could change.

I also tried to do all I could to help salvage the character's manhood, but I couldn't change the story lines. I knew that my efforts to protect the character, for the sake of the narrative about *Men*, could compromise my position with the leadership of the show and could cost me my job, but I fervently believed it was the sacrifice that Christ would have made without hesitation. He is *my* model, and I gladly mirror him!

There are other *Men* who helped father me in the dynamic ways of "being first." Dr. Martin Luther King Jr., Malcolm X, and Muhammad Ali all had to do what was difficult. Taking a stand is, sooner or later, something every righteous being is called to do. Dr. King took a stand against racial inequality. Using his faith and intellect to battle his enemies, he knew he would be putting his life at great risk. Malcolm X is one of the greatest examples of manhood transformation—from serving time to serving the masses and clinging so hard to his faith that he took a stand, not only against racism, but against the hypocrisy of his own leader and teacher. And Muhammad Ali literally put his purpose over profit. He easily could have chosen to use his fame as his fortune but instead chose to live as a righteous servant of the people and be the "people's champion." In 1967, Ali stood against a government that wanted him to fight in a war he knew to be unjust and unwarranted.

All of these *Men* served as great examples of unwavering manhood, as the kind of *Men* our society desperately needs. They are the surrogate fathers who helped shape the purpose-driven *Man* I am today.

It is vitally important for us to be first, because most of our communities have given up on us, based on what they have experienced from our male counterparts. Because of physical appearance, grown males are often mistaken for us. They usually lack the mental and emotional fortitude and the spiritual compass that we as *Men* share and exemplify daily. "Being first" was the example that brothers King, X, and Ali represented to me. And I, as a *Man*, always want to dedicate myself to the practice of being first. My stand is not a knock against any one person or group of people in particular, but I can't overstate the fact that we are truly in need of a better understanding of the difference between a grown male and a *Man*.

BEING FIRST AT HOME

As *Men*, we must *be first* everywhere we go, but particularly in our homes. I have already explained why I do not curse or use foul language as a practice. I believe it is the vocabulary of pain. It's the kind of language that often keeps us stuck in a space of hardheartedness. I also believe it's my obligation to "be first" in using speech absent of obscenities with my family. No great foundation of intimacy is built on using the vocabulary of pain.

I do not use that language in my house because I do not want my wife and children to use it. I do not use it with my wife because I am trying to build great intimacy with her. Even if she doesn't acknowledge it or is unaware of it, my use of a loving vocabulary in her presence communicates that I am seeking a certain level of respect for the beautiful being God created. If I were to use explicit language with her, something in her spirit would say, *Wow,*

I'm missing a shelter of protection and respect from my husband. That language does not cover my heart!

Even if she never communicates that thought, I know it makes a significant difference. Being the first to communicate well in my family establishes the pathway for the family and the way we will interact with each other. Again, being first is setting a course for change in our trajectory. While I do not judge anyone for using that vocabulary, it has been my observation that too often it is associated with great pain. Nevertheless, many people have chosen explicit language and obscenities as a chief mode of communication.

I talk to many men who are disgruntled in their current relationships about many issues. I advise my brothers that the way to get a particular kind of behavior changed in their significant other is to "be first" in modeling *positive* behaviors. The ones who heed my advice find themselves in better relationships, sometimes in as little as a couple of weeks.

The Word teaches us that "a gentle answer turns away wrath."[1] Therefore, responding at volume ten to someone yelling at you at volume seven is going to escalate your discussion into a fight. However, if your spouse is engaging in conversation with you at volume seven and you respond at volume four, more often than not, you will find the situation begin to de-escalate.

I often use an analogy to help my brothers visualize where they should be with this technique. When you were learning to drive, your instructor said to you, "Keep your hands on the wheel at the ten o'clock position and the two o'clock position. For you to stay in control of the vehicle, your hands should remain at ten and two." Well, think of your relationship, your marriage, as the vehicle, and think of your partner's speaking or addressing you at volume ten. For you to remain in control, you have to respond to her at volume two. If your partner speaks to you in a way you know is inviting an argument, as the leader of your house, you have to find a way to model the way you want her to further engage you. In other words, "be first" by changing the response. If she yells at you at volume ten, respond to her gently at volume two.

When you speak to someone at volume two and they are speaking at volume ten, they have to lower their volume in order to hear you. Furthermore, it is quite difficult for anyone to continue to yell when you are not. Eventually, any sane person will begin to recognize that they are the only ones engaged in less than righteous behavior and will either behave differently or remove themselves from the environment.

Remember that we should perform as servant leaders, not by telling people what to do, but by showing people what to do.

As *Men*, we must have the kind of discipline that denies our flesh, which is trying to tell us to prove that we are the "stronger" one and that we must get the other person to bend to our physical will. Our flesh will tell us to yell. But we have to begin to master the practice of modeling righteous behavior. We can only accomplish this by "being first."

Please know I am not naive. I certainly know that some of us have chosen a life partner who will challenge this method. Also, some of those situations may require some counseling and a little more spiritual work, but we are required to keep trying. Remember that we should perform as servant leaders, not by *telling* people what to do, but by *showing* people what to do. You may have a partner who yells constantly. What took many years for her to learn will take some diligent time to unlearn and then to learn new behaviors. Remember that she has the right to struggle, just like you did and may still be doing.

RETHINKING YOUR REACTIONS

Next I want to encourage you to rethink your interactions and reactions. This turnaround is not always easy to do, but it is essential for every *Man*, since "being first" starts with looking at our "being first"! We have to examine our spirits to figure out whether what we are "being first" in is good for our households and our communities. And being open to the loving accountability of others is a huge part of that. That is why my friend and brother Hasani Pettiford often says, "Every *Man* needs a *Man*!"

I believe we can better practice the mantra of "being first" when we have more patience. We have to be patient in order to help people identify their shortcomings and lead them in a righteous direction. All of this starts with self. When we can identify our own shortcomings and realize we have more baggage than we care to admit, we can empathize with other people's shortcomings and remain patient as we seek clarity to lead by "being first."

For instance, in Matthew 7:3–5, Jesus admonishes us, "Why do you look at the speck of sawdust in your brother's eye and pay no attention to the plank in your own eye? How can you say to your brother, 'Let me take the speck out of your eye,' when all the time there is a plank in your own eye? You hypocrite, first take the plank out of your own eye, and then you will see clearly to remove the speck from your brother's eye." This passage is a powerful reminder that we constantly need to extract the spiritual planks from our eyes before calling out the specks in the eyes of our brothers.

When we become proficient at doing this, we are better equipped to practice "being first." People will trust us and follow us because they know that the true nature of our character is to be someone who routinely looks for the plank in our own eye so we can lead others to the best of our ability.

Jesus' admonishment serves as our model, and it will elevate our own manhood. Jesus was always using thought-provoking metaphors and parables to convey transformation to his followers. It's easy to look at someone else and begin to rattle off a list of things he or she needs to do differently and come up with ways to transform them, but how do we transform ourselves *first*? How do we mindfully execute "being first" in the area of self-transformation?

Jesus makes another powerful statement in Matthew 18:3. In a conversation with his disciples, they asked him, "Who is the greatest in the kingdom of heaven?" His answer was simple and profound. Jesus pointed to a nearby child and responded, "Unless you change and become like little children, you will never enter the kingdom of heaven." This seems basic, but it is so integral to the lesson: we need to be the fully realized men we were ordained to be. The currency of the kingdom is *faith*. Jesus is suggesting that we need to have faith like a child who has not been tainted by the world and its cynicism, that we should seek the perfection of our spirit and rebuke the things that have allowed us to become distant from God.

Additionally, we need to have the humility of a child. Now I know many of you are saying, "Kids today are not humble!" That may be true, but let's ask why. We have been the ones who have been "first" in modeling for them a lack of humility. So to change them is to change us. Whenever my children do something I don't like, I have to change the way I engage it—I have to rethink my reaction. I used to immediately blame them, but now the first question I ask myself is, *Have I done something that gives their behavior permission to exist?*

This is difficult to do at times because it requires us to examine ourselves constantly and to take responsibility for things that go on around us. Hence, the difference between a grown male and a *Man* emerges. But remember, as a *Man*, you will be asked to endure more hardships than most can handle, and your flesh will be tempted to take the wheel.

Honestly speaking, it's pretty tough to be humble when someone has activated our flesh by bringing trauma into our lives or even simply by making us feel bad. We immediately want to lash out at the person and make him or her feel as bad as we've been made to feel. It would seem that the more we deny our flesh, the more qualified we are for "being first" and leading.

Jesus says to us in the Bible that humility and willingness to change are requirements for citizenship in the kingdom. Leaning on our own strength is one of the hopes of the enemy. We have to truly lean into our ultimate power source. God wants what is best for us and has every intention to facilitate growth for us. Knowing that God has us in mind allows us to avoid feeling isolated. Left to our own devices, we will drop the proverbial ball every time. We need God in order to want to "be first." We need to have the accountability of a higher source and our brothers to mature so that we become an ally and not an adversary to our community, an asset and not a liability to our people.

So again, each time we begin to examine others, we should always wind up back at ourselves. If we continue to use this approach in our lives, we will be equipped for the task of "being first."

CHAPTER 7

GOD + DO = SUCCESSFUL LIFE

Although I have been an actor for more than three decades and have been afforded the opportunity to experience and see many things, I have two memories that trump all the rest—the memories of my children taking their first steps.

I understand why Jesus was always admonishing his listeners to have the faith and demeanor of a child. Children forgive freely, love lavishly, and have the power to forget, which in turn activates a powerful faith. You see, my children, like many of yours and like our own experiences as children, stumbled and bumped into furniture and even hurt themselves while testing out this concept of walking; however, they never gave up *trying* to walk. This directly mirrors life. We are constantly trying to walk it out without bumping into the furniture. The obstacles, despite our knowledge of their existence in our environment, will still cause us to stumble.

I love the fact that when we are younger, we don't give up on something just because it doesn't work for us the first time. It is truly incredible that before anyone ever teaches us how to meditate or pray, we have an understanding that God has empowered us to do great things. It makes perfect sense, doesn't it? We were created in his image, so it makes sense that we have been supernaturally wired to do great and mighty things.

Unfortunately, as we grow up, depending on the words that are fed to us, we may no longer be convinced that we are completely capable of getting back up again after falling. We may have been

121

robbed of the confidence to seek God on our second, fourth, or forty-fourth attempt at something, but I am here to bring you good news.

YOUR DO

God has endowed you with everything you need to win. All you have to do is remind yourself of the intention behind your creation and combine it with your "do"—in other words, your actions. The New Testament book of James breaks it down this way:

> What good is it, my brothers, if someone says he has faith but does not have works? Can that faith save him? If a brother or sister is poorly clothed and lacking in daily food, and one of you says to them, "Go in peace, be warmed and filled," without giving them the things needed for the body, what good is that? So also faith by itself, if it does not have works, is dead.
>
> But someone will say, "You have faith and I have works." Show me your faith apart from your works, and I will show you my faith by my works. You believe that God is one; you do well. Even the demons believe—and shudder! Do you want to be shown, you foolish person, that faith apart from works is useless? Was not Abraham our father justified by works when he offered up his son Isaac on the altar? You see that faith was active along with his works, and faith was completed by his works; and the Scripture was fulfilled that says, "Abraham believed God, and it was counted to him as righteousness"—and he was called a friend of God. You see that a person is justified by works and not by faith alone. And in the same way was not also Rahab the prostitute justified

by works when she received the messengers and sent them out by another way? For as the body apart from the spirit is dead, so also faith apart from works is dead.[1]

This is a powerful commentary. James is strongly suggesting for our consideration that apart from our works, our faith means very little. Our belief in the God of heaven, in concert with the energy and effort we put forth, leads us to live our best lives.

I can explain how this relates to acting. When I talk to strangers and friends alike who audition for characters and tell me they don't believe they got the part, I am always intrigued as to why they feel that way. Shockingly, many of them express the belief that God did not mean for them to have the job or get the part.

By now you know I have somewhat of a probing nature, so I always ask them, "Why don't you think God meant for you to have it?" That inquiry almost always leads me to ask another question: "What does your preparation look like?"

Usually based on the answers, I conclude that they may not have studied the character, researched the part, or learned the lines as thoroughly as they could have; however, almost always, the person absolutely insists that they earnestly *prayed* for the role but did not adequately *prepare* for the role. More specifically, they diligently *prayed* to get the job but did not diligently *work* to get the job.

Now, this is fascinating to me, not because I am not a believer—I am; nor is it because I am not a *Man* of faith and prayer—I am. It is fascinating because when God gives us an opportunity, the prayer portion has already been answered; now it is time for us to do the work. This is the "free will" part of living a life of faith. The "God's will" portion of life is us having the opportunity; the "free will" portion of life is what we do with the opportunity.

There is prayer, and there is also work. The key to unlocking the next level in your life, the key to upgrading your life from "good" to "great" or from "great" to "extraordinary," is the part *that God will do for you*. Still, there is an important part *that you must do for yourself*! Without that "you do," you don't!

In the end, as important as it is to pray and have faith, we must never forget that God instructs us to be "doers." Again from the book of James:

> But be doers of the word, and not hearers only, deceiving your-selves. For if anyone is a hearer of the word and not a doer, he is like a man observing his natural face in a mirror; for he observes himself, goes away, and immediately forgets what kind of man he was. But he who looks into the perfect law of liberty and continues in it, and is not a forgetful hearer but a doer of the work, this one will be blessed in what he does.[2]

For instance, when presented with opportunities to win roles over a thirty-five-year career, I seldom lacked confidence to obtain those roles because I was prepared to ace each opportunity— studying those lines so I knew the dialogue backward and forward, which ensured that I could focus on the emotional pitch of the scene; figuring out the intention of the character in the scene; and finally, committing to the scene with all of my focus and energy without fear of failing.

We can apply this approach to more than just acting. It can be applied to everything in life! Notably, it can be applied to the many crises we may face in life. God will equip us. God will give us the opportunity, but because he also gave us free will, we will need to take a certain level of action to find our destiny.

Additionally, God will send us people who serve as conduits for his guidance. These are people we can follow who provide us with important instruction as we battle with temptations to misuse our free will. We all struggle at one point or another with attempting to create a plan "better" than the one God has provided. Something that lessens the temptation to use our free will in a self-destructive manner is good leadership—the people God sends our way.

RECEIVING GOD'S BLESSINGS

When Moses and the newly freed Hebrew slaves got to the Red Sea, they had a choice. They could have said to Moses, "You know, if God is powerful enough to part the sea, he should also be power-ful enough to levitate us to the other side instead of us having to walk between walls of water." Fortunately, they trusted Moses and God in this instance. They followed Moses across the seabed and escaped the Egyptians.[3]

Most of the biggest blessings in your life will take great work to come to fruition. Moses led the way while the people partici-pated in their own "freedom journey." This is important because often people want God to "miracle" them out of a difficult situa-tion. They want to use God as a genie in a lamp or a "get out of jail free" card. Mature and experienced believers know that God does not work that way.

For instance, I look for my kids to demonstrate that they are prepared to receive the blessings that I, as their earthly father, have prepared for them to receive.

We can be only a fraction of the parent God is to us. So some-times we're tempted to look at God as a magical being who will perform hocus-pocus for us. But the truth is that God knows that if he gave us everything we asked for, we would never be prepared to care for the blessings properly. Ultimately, we would squander them or use them to our demise and the demise of those around us. Many of us are doing this with the blessings we have right now. God is the ultimate parent who is looking to bless us when he recognizes that we are prepared to steward the blessing he intends for us.

God provides for us but then requires a level of work to be done to maintain the blessing that is given. Anyone who has a vehicle understands this process. If you purchase a car but don't do the work required to pay for the car each month, you will not have the car long. Putting in strategic work allows us to retain our blessings, unlike treating God like a lottery system and expecting to give a little cash for a huge windfall. As crazy as it may sound, I know people who want to live in constant celebration without adequate preparation, and that is not a good long-term strategy. You may be able to celebrate some small wins without significant preparation, but you will not be able to endure throughout time and sustain a life of success.

It's just like the sports team that starts undefeated but chooses not to sustain the level of energy and effort that got them to that point in the first place. They end up falling behind or falling short.

COURTSIDE LESSONS

I help coach all of my kids' sports teams, and the one thing I stress to them is constant energy and effort. Recently, I coached my son's basketball team in a two-day tournament. The Saturday games were blowouts! The boys ran through their competition as if those teams had never played the game before. Our team played with energy and effort and executed with great precision. The game seemed to be simple—in fact, almost rudimentary! The boys left the gym feeling like champions, and they deserved to feel that way based on how they played those two games. We stressed to them that tomorrow would be a new day and they would need to reset and come out with renewed attention.

The next day, my son asked, "Dad, what time is the championship game?" And I simply but sternly replied, "Son, you guys have to win the semifinal game *first*." He had a look on his face that told me he had underestimated the significance of the first game we needed to win to get to the championship game. We got to the gym, and unfortunately, his teammates seemed to have the same look in their eyes and shared the same sentiments. They were all quite confident—okay, let's say it, they were overconfident, and it showed.

The tip-off came, and right from the beginning, our team was dominated. Not because the other team was the better team, but because they had better energy and effort. They outworked us and executed consistently enough to hand us the worst defeat of the season—a twenty-point loss tied entirely to the fact that we lacked the secret ingredients of just one day prior: energy and effort. We were thoroughly outworked on both offense and defense, and by the time the boys tried to make an adjustment, it was too late because the lead was too much to recover from and time ran out.

Without energy and effort, no matter how knowledgeable or skilled we are, we will be unable to execute properly and will invite failure to step into our lives. I often—well, actually, always—tell my kids that their success on the basketball court, the softball/baseball field, or the golf course can be directly tied to their energy and effort. There will always be someone who is more talented than you are. As an individual or as a team, the secret ingredients to over-coming those seemingly insurmountable odds are, you guessed it,

Without energy and effort, no matter how knowledgeable or skilled we are, we will be unable to execute properly and will invite failure to step into our lives.

energy and effort. You cannot control whether you compete against someone who is more skilled than you are, but you can control whether you allow them to outwork you. That is something we all have control over, yet many of us choose to forfeit that portion of our lives.

Let me put it to you this way: if God loves us all equally and seeks to bless us all, then the things that most determine the ulti-mate outcomes in life are our preparedness and the energy and effort applied to that preparation. It is just that simple.

When we do as our basketball team did and allow ourselves to live in the celebration moments more than the preparation moments, rather than leaning into our endurance and consistency, our wins will cease.

This happens to believers far too often because we avoid putting in consistent work. As believers, we will sometimes work for something and then mistakenly think that God should take over because he loves us. Unfortunately, the genuinely lasting accomplishments in life come from sustained physical work. This energy and effort cannot be supplanted by the spiritual exchange between God and us. A space of consistent success and achieve-ment is an exchange between the work put forth by humans and the empowerment of the triune God in the heavens.

To further prove my point about how important our "do" is, think about all the accomplished people you know who do not have a healthy and sustained relationship with God. There are many in popular culture. How did they get to those spaces of accomplishment if they have no real relationship with God? Simple. They *do*. They work! You can be extremely accomplished in your line of work without God, but the key for me to having a balance of accomplishment and the true measurements of success—a healthy family and home life with purpose—is through God.

BE A DOER

My acting teacher in high school always said to us, "Acting is doing!" He told us that to mirror life on the screen or in front of an audience, we had to be in a constant state of doing. He further explained that we needed to figure out what our character's intention was in the scene we were executing.

In life, our intention as *Men* should always be to have sustained energy and effort, to execute the way we are expected to. In other words, *do*! In this time when males are mistaken for *Men* based on their physical characteristics, being a *Man* is one of the toughest jobs anyone can ever expect to execute. We have to remember that manhood is tied to being a servant to others.

However, being a *Man* also requires us to be stern enough to enforce the rules and provide necessary boundaries for our family. We also must be sensitive enough to be vulnerable with our loved ones and not hide our humanity. Manhood must be transparent enough to admit when we are wrong and not pretend we are perfect, humble enough to remember we are not God (that job is already taken), and spiritual enough to mirror Jesus Christ as our model. Just as Christ was a "doer," we must be as well. Simultaneously, we have to ask God to send us blessings in the way of opportunities we will honor with our energy and effort so we can execute in a way that will make him proud.

Manhood must be transparent enough to admit when we are wrong and not pretend we are perfect, humble enough to remember we are not God, and spiritual enough to mirror Jesus Christ as our model.

I cannot stress enough the "doer" portion of our walk. It is so vital to who we are for ourselves, but just as important, it is what we are always to model for everyone who falls under our coverage. While Christ is our model, we have the assignment of being the earthly model everyone else can mirror. I have to keep stressing this, because it is at the core of our spiritual assignment. If we are dynamically dedicated to this assignment, those around us should be true reflections of a "doer"!

THE MATH OF JAMES

Remember James's instructions? "But be doers of the word, and not hearers only . . . But he who looks into the perfect law of liberty and continues in it, and is not a forgetful hearer but a doer of the work, this one will be blessed in what he does" (James 1:22–25 NKJV).

If we were mathematicians trying to write an equation for a successful life, it would simply look like this:

GOD + DO = SUCCESSFUL LIFE

Combine faith and actions. Be hearers and doers of the word. This, indeed, has been one of the most effective equations I've used for cultivating a greatly successful life.

CHAPTER 8

"HAPPY WIFE,
HAPPY LIFE"

As you know, *Man* U is about all things *Man* related. I wanted to touch on a subject that rarely gets covered in discussions with men about their relationships. It is one of the biggest reasons we men fall short of certain marks within the confines of our relationships, but specifically in our marriages.

In my humble but informed opinion, based on my counseling of couples, "happy wife, happy life" is a phrase that gets many committed relationships into trouble. I truly dislike this phrase as used by society. It sets up unrealistic expectations for men to live up to and also sets up women to be let down when their expectations aren't met. A husband who has this assignment can never live up to this expectation. A wife will always be let down because no husband will ever be able to live up to what society claims he should be.

Let us start with the truth that no one ever wants to deal with: *we as individuals have the assignment of making ourselves happy and bringing that happiness to the marriage.*

Many Bible teachers use the word *helpmate* to describe how men and women should serve each other in marriage.[1] As we saw with Adam and Eve, God intended that we would have a companion and helper in life. As helpmates, we have the assignment of *accentuating* each other's happiness. Notice that I used the word *accentuating*, not *providing*. In order for something to be accentuated, it must already exist; to provide something means it does not. To accentuate something means we make what exists *better*; to provide something means we bring what does not exist into existence.

Plainly speaking, we can make our helpmate *happier*, but making them happy is a myth. It is simply not possible to *make* someone else happy. If you have ever been in a relationship with someone who was unhappy and they seemed to be "happy" when they were with you, their happiness was not truly authentic. They were *distracted* from their unhappiness. While they were distracted, they did not feel the pain of their unfulfilled happiness. They associated the distraction with happiness, and since they experience the relief from their pain of being unhappy when they were with you, they associated you with happiness. This is how people arrive at the place of "he makes me happy" or "she makes me happy."

As helpmates, we have the assignment of accentuating each other's happiness.

DISTRACTED WIFE, LABORED LIFE

When you choose a partner who has not done the diligent work of making herself happy, the very best you can do is have a "distracted wife, labored life." Distracting your wife is going to be a lifetime labor that will never be fulfilled. Each day, you will kill yourself trying to "make her happy," and each day she will come up with a laundry list of things she thinks will make her happy when you fulfill those expectations.

Now do not get this confused. She will feel good because you are committing acts of great service, but that feeling will be short-lived because the root of her unhappiness comes from a much deeper place. No matter what you do, you will never be able to access that place. Her momentary distraction feels good to her to the extent that she feels happy, but honestly, she is not.

There is a particular reason I wanted this chapter to be titled "Happy Wife, Happy Life." Through the following pages, I will explain how, when a *Man* truly covers his wife and children as he is supposed to, the phrase "happy wife, happy life" can be one of the most loving phrases ever uttered.

REAL TOGETHERNESS

The saying "happy wife, happy life," used loosely in society as it is, validates the idea that a husband's happiness does not matter as much as his wife's happiness. It suggests that the only thing that does matter in the marriage is the wife and her feelings and that somehow if the wife is made to "feel" happy, her husband will magically feel happy as well. (I'm laughing out loud because I've been married for more than twenty years, and I know this is categorically incorrect.)

However, I want to encourage brothers to *redefine* their opinion of true happiness. When a male makes the conscious choice to be a *Man*, marriage moves into a partnership, which, by definition, means that *both partners matter*. Yes, #BothPartnersMatter. God says in Hebrews 13:4 (ESV), "Let marriage be held in honor among all, and let the marriage bed be undefiled." Marriage is meant to be about two partners making a conscious choice daily to create a happy life *together*. It cannot just be focused on one person's happiness. If it centers around one person being happy, guess what? The other person in the equation is going to be unhappy!

So the commitment of two people to be happy and walk together is the definition of real togetherness. And if a couple commits to be together through the sanctity of marriage, it means we have to address each other's happiness.

DOING THE WORK
AND PREPARING YOURSELF

Relationships, especially marriage, can test everything we know about ourselves, our partners, and the reason we got married in the first place. The daily issues of life challenge our commitments at their core.

Recently I discussed with a woman—let's call her Tanya—her belief that "marriages are made in heaven." She had been constantly attracted to the wrong types of males and could not understand why God would keep bringing them to her. I felt it was important to debunk the myth that God was the one who sent her this particular partner—or any other male for that matter. I told her in all honesty, "I don't believe God works that way. I don't believe God sits on his throne and says, 'I am going to send Michael into the elevator, and now Tanya is going to walk into the elevator, and now they are going to see each other, fall in love, and live happily ever after.'"

Instead, the truth behind the words "marriages are made in heaven" in my opinion is that God asks all of us to bring *our best selves* to the dating relationship based on the things we know are kingdom expectations. These characteristics of righteousness will eventually produce the marriage we seek. But what are the kingdom expectations?

God gives us each free will, and he expects us to use it well to attract the partner we have asked for through prayer. When living out our faith, or as I say, "walking it out" on earth, it's our job to make sure we always bring our best self to the table to attract the best partner for us. The free will is the "doing" part of life as mentioned in the last chapter. We cannot just pray for a partner; we have to send signals to God that we are truly ready for the partner we wish to be joined with by being the kind of person who genuinely complements who we are. Our "doing" serves further as a beacon that attracts the partner we are prepared to handle. Pay close attention to this. We don't get the partner we want, but rather the partner we are!

When God created us, it was his intention that we would walk out our marriage in this way. However, some individuals struggle with finding the right marriage partner because they've chosen not to do the work on themselves to attract the right partner. That was the case for Tanya. She found herself continually attracting males who were not yet their best selves. And Tanya had chosen not to do the necessary work to become her best self before entering the dating arena. I do not believe there are coincidences; there are only incidences that coincide. In other words, because she did not do the work of preparing herself for a relationship, she attracted partners who were not prepared for relationships either.

Aside from the work she needed to do on herself, I began to talk to her about how to better choose a partner. She said she simply wasn't attracted to "nice guys who seem to be family guys." I submitted to her that she was not attracted to those *Men* because she knew she would eventually have to look at herself in the mirror and begin to challenge the very deficiencies from which she was suffering—a reminder that everything comes back to the work we do on ourselves. Instead, it was easier for her to continue to choose partners who were in the same emotional space she was in because she knew they would never challenge her growth. It was an eye-opening conversation for Tanya that served as a catalyst for her real work to begin.

Tanya was now open to learning about why she seemed to be, in her words, "always attracted to jerks." My answer was a little hard for her to hear at first but necessary. I said to her, "I'm beginning to think your dad may have been a male with poor communication skills and that he treated you and your mom in the same manner as the guys you are attracted to."

As we talked more in-depth, we disclosed that was indeed the case. Her father had been a bit harsh and at times dogmatic in his approach to things, and his behavior impacted her. In reality, he was what many people would describe as "a jerk."

A girl's first love is typically her father. If a girl's father portrayed unhealthy characteristics, when she becomes a woman and starts looking for a marriage relationship, she will typically respond in one of two ways. Either she will be attracted to the familiar (if her father was unkind to her, she will likewise be attracted to those who are unkind to her), or she will purposely choose a *Man* who exhibits the exact opposite characteristics of her father.

These things are crucial to understand. The relationship between a daughter and her father is the dress rehearsal for her future relationships with the opposite sex and, ultimately, the marriage she will seek for herself. I myself struggle to remain mindful of this and intentional about having loving exchanges with my own daughter.

For Tanya, that space of being attracted to a jerk reminded her of the "love" she received from her dad. Consequently, she found herself not attracted to *Men* who were "nice" and who, by her definition, seemed to be "marriage material." To change her mind-set, Tanya first had to acknowledge that she was attracted to the qualities her father demonstrated and that he had set the bar for what she looked for in a partner. Only when she acknowledged that fact could she begin to lay out a different blueprint for the new characteristics that could become attractive to her.

Repentance is the spiritual application of the changing of our mind, and the heart change will soon follow. Tanya was able to reprogram her thoughts to *I am not attracted to males with jerk tendencies. The reason I became attracted to those types of males is that their actions reminded me of how it felt to interact with my father, and I was attracted to what was familiar, not necessarily to what is good for me.* When Tanya took that first step, the other steps to a healthy relationship could soon follow.

She then wrote a list of all the behaviors and characteristics she did find attractive—a "checklist of attrac-

> *Repentance is the spiritual application of the changing of our mind, and the heart change will soon follow.*

tion behaviors." Now when Tanya comes into contact with a *Man* who demonstrates those behaviors, she is able to recall what her true attraction is and begin to walk out a relationship with a *Man* who displays the attributes she truly admires and who will cover her like the tree she should have. Her heart changed because her mind changed.

After all of that, I asked Tanya about her passions and her purpose in life. She asked, "Aren't they the same?" I told her there were subtle but distinct differences between the two, just as is true for males and *Men*—they have the same anatomy, but *Men* have a different intentionality, which makes them the greater version of a male.

Passions and purpose are similar. Passions are things we love to do, while purpose is what we were meant to do that we love. She discovered she did not know these differences—most people don't—and she said, "Truthfully, I don't think I've ever given this much thought." Can you imagine how unfulfilled she felt every day, questioning what her life meant and why she was put on this earth? It left her not only asking more questions than she had answers to, but also knowing she needed to find those answers to access a life of fulfillment and unlock her true happiness. It also let her know that her happiness was not going to be provided by a partner, a helpmate.

Now why is this relevant to us? Because we can learn a lot from the male who has jerk tendencies. He serves as the anti–role model we need to remind us of the version of ourselves we were not intended to be. He serves as an example of how we can contribute to the vicious cycle that happens to women when they are not properly covered and cared for. Tanya further serves as an example of what happens to us when we avoid doing the work that will transform us. She and her father are valuable examples demonstrating that we cannot make a woman happy if she is unhappy with herself. Their story also shows that men play a massive role in the lives of their daughters, who will eventually use that relationship as the measuring stick for their marriage.

A WIFE'S HIDDEN PURPOSE IS TO STRETCH HER HUSBAND

In a healthy marriage, a wife will sometimes give her husband pushback. Traditionally speaking, a *male* thinks a wife should do as she is told and submit to all of his wishes and ways. But marriage is a partnership, and in a partnership, each partner is supposed to give to the marriage what it needs. In Proverbs 27:17, we read, "As iron sharpens iron, so one person sharpens another." Sometimes that isn't going to be met with an agreeing gesture. Sometimes your wife will give pushback that is going to irritate you to the degree that you want to retaliate.

Your job as a mature *Man* is to make sure you see the push-back for what it is—a character-building exercise that allows you to "work out" by executing good character traits in your home so that everything presented to you outside your home will seem easy in comparison. Let's face it, your wife is the only person who can push your buttons in a way that no one else can. Why? Because only she knows exactly what makes you tick. So every time your wife presents pushback, if you view it as the character-building exercise that it is, you are being given *an opportunity* to become a better version of yourself and thus to grow as a *Man*. This push-back is nutrition for us, but we rarely—or never—had it labeled that way for us, even by most of our elders. But we can begin to see our wives as a nutrient and not a nuisance! My wife is truly the nutrient that makes me say, "If you master partnering with your wife, you can master dealing with your life."

I was counseling a married couple, and the husband was complaining to me that his wife was nagging him about his body because she felt he was losing himself. He was getting out of shape, and she admitted she didn't find that aspect attractive. His response to her came from a space of anger produced by his profound pain at her honesty.

I merely asked him a question: "Do you feel it is part of your wife's job description to keep you 'out of the streets'?" This is a saying that refers to preventing the seeking out of sexual partnerships outside the marriage.

He replied, "Yes."

I countered. "So if we know that's the case, then you have to further agree that it is likewise your job to keep your wife 'out of the streets.' You presented yourself to her while you were courting as a fit person. She was physically attracted to you. But things changed over time, and now you're not as fit as you used to be. But you should try to honor your wife by giving your best effort to being more physically fit—to being a version of yourself that she can look forward to coming home to."

The room suddenly got real quiet.

I gave him the following advice: "Begin to address your diet. Your wife has been trying to encourage you to become vegan. At the very least, look at it as a way to prevent toxins from entering your body and as a way to fight against the toxins that currently exist. This will allow you to address your health and to rightfully submit to your wife as the helpmate who cares for you. I want you to submit in the way that God wants all of us to do with our helpmates and allow her to cook for you and feed you medicine that will begin to heal up your body, and in turn it will help you become more physically fit, which will be more attractive to her. Not only will it produce better physical and health results, but it will also send her signals that you are a God-honoring *Man* who is strong enough to do what grown males are afraid to do: *submit*."[2] Now that's not to suggest that being vegan is the only way to be healthy, but through submitting to his wife's love, care, and counsel, their marriage went to a higher place. And he was able to make her *happier* by being the *Man* he was intended to be.

THE HIDDEN OPPORTUNITY IN EACH CHALLENGE

As a *Man* who is given the responsibility to cover my wife, each time I receive pushback from her, I have the opportunity to demonstrate the qualities of collaboration, empathy, and gentleness—all cushioned under the umbrella of love. As a human being made of flesh, I don't always achieve this or perfectly walk it out. But it is the intention that I pursue perfectly. And when I demonstrate these qualities consistently, I build up our marriage and do my part to help create a happier life for both of us. In the following paragraphs, I will break down these three characteristics with easy-to-understand examples.

Collaboration

A great example of being collaborative every day is the idea of asking my wife what she thinks about specific decisions that need to be made for our family. Even when I know I have the answer, I try to make sure I engage her as a helpmate. It's not about whether I'm capable of making a decision or making the correct decision; it boils down instead to continually sending a signal to my wife that we are partners in every sense of the word. Biblically speaking, 1 Corinthians 1:10 (ESV) talks about this very concept: "I appeal to you, brothers, by the name of our Lord Jesus Christ, that all of you agree, and that there be no divisions among you, but that you be united in the same mind and the same judgment." The following example is a way to take that biblical principle and apply it proactively.

I would say something like this: "Hey, sweetheart, we have to figure out how Dré is going to get to his basketball tournament because we're both gone that weekend. I thought Timothy's parents could take him, but I didn't want to make that decision myself in case you had another plan. What would you like to do?"

Now I'm fairly certain that Timothy's parents are an obvious choice because we both trust them, and I further know she will probably agree with that decision. But my question is not about whether I know who should take our son to his tournament. The message I am driving home to her is that she is my partner and I want to collaborate with her on the decision that ultimately gets made. This particular decision may seem unimportant, but it affects our children, which affects us both. I am letting her know daily that she matters by considering her opinion in things that affect us both. This in turn opens her up to be more attracted to me, which ultimately brings us closer to each other in our marriage. I was able to use an ordinary daily decision—a pretty simple one, in fact—to help build our marriage bond.

Empathy

My wife knows I have become a *Man* who does not use foul language. That is my choice. However, my wife will sometimes go into autopilot and use language that can deactivate me at best and infuriate me at worst.

As previously mentioned, I describe that language as "the vocabulary of pain." It's language that one usually wouldn't engage in unless triggered by an external pain—physically, emotionally, or psychologically.

Empathy is looking at why my wife is using language that doesn't activate me in a good way, that might shut me down. Instead of judging my wife for using the language, I choose to figure out what happened to her during the day that would trigger her pain. In 1 Thessalonians 5:11, we're instructed to "encourage one another and build each other up."

I will then listen to her as she tells me about how frustrating her day was. I am now able to recognize she was tested, as we all are, by her flesh, and those particular events led her to use negative language. She knows the vocabulary of pain does not make me feel good, so her using it would have to come from a pretty hurtful experience. I can choose to realize that her choice of words isn't about me, but instead is more about the pain produced by her day. Then I can choose to become a servant to help relieve the stress and strain of what she had to endure during the week instead of shutting down or making it about me. Now, again, we are never going to be perfect, but our job is to constantly pursue perfection.

Gentleness

In Philippians 4:5, we read, "Let your gentleness be evident to all." In this portion of this exercise, I use gentle language and actions to send messages to my wife that what she is doing may not be her best—and to do this without judging, arguing, or condemning. I can choose my words, tone, and physical touch to convey what I want for our partnership in that moment and to gently point out what I would like to address.

As a *Man*, I have to try to be gentle in all of my communications, particularly expressions of hurt, frustration, passion, and irritation. These are challenges we all face, but it is our responsibility to undertake them daily. Not only do they expand our manhood, but as always, they model for our environment what we want mirrored.

> *As a Man, I have to try to be gentle in all of my communications. Doing so not only expands our manhood, but it also models what we want mirrored.*

145

The Loving Umbrella

As the Bible says in 1 Corinthians 13:4–7 (ESV), "Love is patient and kind; love does not envy or boast; it is not arrogant or rude. It does not insist on its own way; it is not irritable or resentful; it does not rejoice at wrongdoing, but rejoices with the truth. Love bears all things, believes all things, hopes all things, endures all things."

To be a *Man* who is a tree for his wife, family, and community, he must make all of those things a living practice. When I consider my wife's feelings regarding a decision I am more than capable of making on my own, when I'm empathetic toward my wife instead of taking her language personally, and when I use gentle language to send signals to better communicate in that moment, all of those techniques encompass the loving behavior that needs to be shown consistently to help build up my marriage. These actions, when combined coherently, help my wife to feel, *Wow, I am the partner my husband says I am, and he is constantly considering me.* These actions help build a strong, happy marriage and, when played out every day, will make her happier.

REAL-WORLD APPLICATION

Below are three examples of how a real-world couple plays out various interactions daily. The first scenario shows how shame can tear a marriage apart; the second scenario shows how a loving response builds a bridge between two partners; and the third scenario shows that even when one partner uses an unhealthy pattern to potentially tear away at the marriage foundation, a healthy response will mend the tear and give the marriage the opportunity to be built up. A *Man* has to find a way to bring the skills of collaboration, empathy, and gentleness into his marriage and home to increase the peace and well-being of his family.

Men like to live in an atmosphere of peace. When a man comes through the door after a long day on the job, he is looking for refuge from the world because he has had to deal with people and problems all day. Yes, we all know women have had to deal with those same issues, but a man's battle in the world is slightly different due to the threat he may pose to others based on his physicality.

For instance, my wife and I are both exposed to highly stressful environments outside our home, but as a man, I will be seen as a threat to some who will not see her as the same threat simply because she is a woman and may be seen as physically weaker and less intimidating. I have to defuse with my countenance and vocabulary each environment I encounter where I know I'm being seen as a threat. Many men experience this daily, and the last thing they want to do is come home to engage in another battle.

Meet Alice and Tom
Scenario #1

When Alice chooses to lead with her flesh, she makes a choice to sabotage the atmosphere of peace in her home.

Alice greets Tom at the door with these words: "I thought I told you yesterday to take out the garbage. And what about fixing the closet? You never listen to anything I say, and that's because you're a jerk."

Now there is a way Alice could activate her husband to give her everything she desires, but Alice isn't choosing wisely. She is instead choosing the learned behavior of *shaming* to try to activate her husband. It doesn't matter if she learned it from her childhood, from television, or from witnessing her girlfriends using it on their husbands. She is now mirroring what she has been shown.

She chooses to shame her husband in the hope that it will motivate him to do what she desires, when in fact it does the opposite and shuts him down. It deactivates him! She is going to have on her hands a combustible argument that will probably end badly. At the very least, some language will be exchanged that will leave her hurt and discouraged—and worst-case scenario, it could escalate to the degree that it becomes physical. We must always recognize that these exchanges may seem simple or meaningless to our wives but can become dire to us if we do not diagnose the potential danger.

Scenario #2

If Alice had used the techniques I described in detail above, her and Tom's evening may have gone more like this.

Alice greets Tom at the door again, only this time she says, "Sweetheart, how was your day? Is there anything I can do for you right now that will allow you to be able to rest and relax?"

Now this catches Tom completely off guard. He wasn't expecting that greeting from his wife at all. In his mind, he is thinking, *Wow, I thought she was going to greet me at the door with more stuff for me to do and turn it into another fight when I've been fighting all day already.*

Instead of becoming defensive, he feels like he matters to the most important person in the world to him. Alice is choosing to act in the way a helpmate is supposed to act, and that is to serve her partner. What she does not realize at this moment is that by serving him, she is summoning up the servant in him.

After she has given Tom time to rest and relax, she can say,

"Sweetheart, I know you have a ton on your plate, and I so appreciate everything you always do. I know you've done enough, but whenever you can, I would love it if we could address the closet. I would love it if we could address the garbage—but again, it's fine to do that when you can."

What she is conveying to Tom is that she trusts him to choose when to do what she is asking of him, and because he wants to please her, if he is truly dedicated to serving as a *Man*, he will probably begin to do it in that very moment. Employing the "do this now or else" tactic usually triggers the fight-or-flight response.

In her language and her service, she honors her marriage and, even better, builds up her marriage while summoning the servant leader in her husband.

Scenario #3

In this example, when the *Man* chooses to cover his wife using the techniques described above, he is making a choice for a happy life.

Alice greets Tom at the door with these words: "I thought I told you yesterday to take out the garbage. And what about fixing the closet? You never listen to anything I say, and that's because you're a jerk."

Tom is taken aback but immediately begins to recognize that Alice is carrying something that has nothing to do with him.

We often think that everything we are receiving is about us. The minute we recognize that what we are being met with doesn't have anything to do with us but has more to do with the other person, we can allow ourselves to be in an empathetic space and be more loving. The minute we feel like it's a personal attack, we are unable to effectively use the above techniques to defuse the situation.

Tom recognizes Alice's words are about her and not about him, so he responds with, "Wow, sweetheart, I apologize for not getting to that sooner. I am a little hurt by the way you expressed what you wanted, but I understand, and I will get to it now because you are my priority. Again, I apologize for the delay."

Using *collaboration*, the message Tom sent to Alice by addressing her needs was that she matters. What is fantastic and key about this exchange is that he takes responsibility for his lack of execution. He further uses *gentleness* when addressing the fact that she might not have shown up in a way that nourishes their partnership. By offering an *empathetic* voice, along with empathetic action, a *Man* can always help build up his marriage.

THE TRUE DEFINITION OF "HAPPY WIFE, HAPPY LIFE"

If each person in the marriage continually says to themselves, *I am in a friendly competition of love every day, and I'm going to outdo my partner in this area*, then what you have on your hands is a loving dynamic relationship that will never die. If each partner said to themselves, *I am the problem and the solution*, they are taking equal share of the responsibility and accepting the task of doing something to fortify the relationship. They become helpmates in making their marriage the kind that God ordained it to be. If each person consciously shows up as their best every single day, their marriage will not just survive but begin to thrive.

Society's definition of "happy wife, happy life" cannot be achieved by merely acting upon her every moan and groan. Let us be reminded that we cannot make anyone happy; we can only make them happier. The happy part is their assignment.

After your wife has accepted the assignment of making herself happy, you as a *Man* can accentuate her happiness by honoring your marriage as you do what you know God would have you do: be loving, gentle, and empathetic, and cover your wife in those areas as a good husband would. She will be happier and more fulfilled, and she will feel genuinely valued and loved. When you consciously take the daily opportunities presented to you to build your marriage, your wife will be happier in her spirit and happier that you are her helpmate. When your wife experiences this version of "happy," you will indeed have a happier life as well. Just remember, be first!

CHAPTER 9

CREATE SAFE
SPACES

In many neighborhoods, one person's home often ends up being the "hang-out spot." I didn't get to experience this much in my own neighborhood growing up due to limited resources—hard days of work just to keep the family financially afloat. As a result, my parents were seldom inspired to deal with additional children by making their small apartment the hang-out spot. However, as I got older and went to high school, I discovered the phenomenon of the neighborhood hang-out spot as I went to friends' homes and experienced the shared space that felt so communal and safe. It was life-changing.

I noticed that the hang-out spot had become so for a myriad of reasons: the person's parents could be the "cool parents" or their house could be well stocked with food and drinks or they could have the latest video games. It didn't matter how their house came to be the hang-out spot—it was well-known to everyone.

My house has turned into that kind of spot for many of my children's friends. My wife and I have intentionally created an atmosphere for our children and their friends to want to come to, and that cannot happen without it feeling like a safe space. Invariably something special happens. As a result of the safety they feel in our home, when our children's friends visit, they often engage us in ways they engage few other parents.

Recently my daughter had some of her former fast-pitch softball teammates at the house for a sleepover. I have served in the capacity of a coach for all of these girls. I work very hard at establishing great bonds with all the kids I coach because I know the invaluable life lessons that can be learned through playing sports. We can carry with us for a lifetime potent and specific lessons that will speak to some of our greatest deficiencies.

Well, when these players come over, they are as eager to spend time with the "coach" (me) as they are with their teammate and friend (my daughter). On this particular sleepover, they had me in the hot seat! They all wanted me to sit with them as they asked questions about what they were currently experiencing and were curious about regarding boys. They asked rapid-fire questions about dating, and every fiber of my being wanted to say, *Noooooooooo. Boys are not prepared to properly care for your heart! Ruuuuuuuuun!*

However, I knew they wouldn't listen to that, so I did what I usually do: I tried to offer them counsel that would help them properly execute their goals, as any good coach would do.

One of the young ladies asked me how to determine if she had found a good guy. Now, again, every adult reading this knows there is only so much good on the mind of a teenage male as it relates to adolescent females, so I knew I needed to share some fundamental truths with them.

DATING ADVICE FROM TREES

The first thing I wanted to discuss was why they thought they needed to have a boyfriend in the first place. I wanted them to know that their counterpart males did not possess the same prefrontal cortex and would often have self-serving motives for dating them—motives that were likely different from the ones the girls would have for dating the boys. As I pointed out the difference in the way the two sexes categorized dating in the teenage years, I could see them sobering up a bit. They were being hit with more than they bargained for, and it was evident.

We often look for things in other people that we are not getting in our own lives. Girls can sometimes use boys as the supplement for male energy and attention that they may not be receiving from their fathers, as a way of seeking a connection with God, or as a way of dealing with the poor image they may have of themselves.

As we talked about these things, I could see their energy begin to wane.

I then walked over to a window, pointed to a tree in my yard, and simply asked them, "What does that tree do?" They all looked at me inquisitively and began to slowly and awkwardly offer answers. I started receiving various responses, and then I expounded upon them.

First, I encouraged them to avoid dating at this age because they were still learning about themselves and because males, particularly teenage males, tend to continually look to be served! It is a rare occasion when males in their teenage years are humble servant leaders who look to serve those around them and are not seeking to feed their flesh. These facts are in stark contrast to what females look for and need in a partner. The first part of my job as a surrogate caretaker and coach was done.

Back to the tree. I suggested that when they knew themselves better and when it was clear that they were looking for lasting companionship, they needed to find a tree. As we said earlier, a *Man* is the tree of his family and his community, with a goal of covering and protecting. A tree is a gift that God provides our environment. It turns the waste we produce into life-giving air, carbon dioxide into oxygen.

Similarly, a mature *Man* has the ability to take things from people that can be harmful and turn them into something that will give life to the recipient. A *Man* has to be like a deeply rooted tree that is immovable for the sake of the family and that takes the toxic nature of what comes at him and turns it into something others around him can use to increase themselves. Trees provide food. The knowledge these girls were seeking is like the food we all need to build ourselves up. A *Man's* words should be like protein that helps build up those around him.

A Man's words should be like protein that helps build up those around him.

Like trees, *Men* have been assigned to provide shelter too. Shelter is the kind of cover that those around them need in order to feel safe from the dangerous elements of the world. If we stood outside under the harmful aspects of the world without the cover of a tree, we would undoubtedly be burned by the sun. Trees are invaluable to their environment, and they provide assets that people around them don't even know they need. A tree offers benefits without you asking, and you receive them without even knowing you are benefiting from the tree.

A *Man*, like a tree, helps people be calm and settled because of the *safe space* he provides.

The awareness was slowly sinking into the girls that the true definition of a companion may be different from what they had thought or been taught. I suggested that the appropriate suitor would present himself as a tree that would make their environment better and not worse, that would add value to their existence and not make life more difficult. "My job as a *Man*, like a tree,"

I said, "is to provide for my family and to provide for all those around me as well."

The talk with the girls went exceptionally well, and it began to dawn on me that we men have much work to do. Just as women were never taught to seek a tree, we were never taught to be a tree. And in so many cases, we allow our unhealed traumas and anger to scorch those around us who are looking to us to create safe spaces. The effects are always devastating. We can avoid that kind of devastation by first realizing that we are intended to be trees that are as strong and tall as giant sequoia trees, providing dependable safety and stability.

MAY I BOARD THE FLIGHT NOW?

I want to tell you a story about something I experienced—a day when my strength as a *Man* was tested.

I was at the airport, flying home after witnessing the graduation of my goddaughter from college. My flight was delayed due to bad weather, so I was waiting in the terminal. In the meantime, I got a call from the mom of one of my mentees. She asked if I could have a talk with him about his focus during one of his upcoming competitions. I sat in the restaurant at the small airport and tried to offer perspective and counsel.

I also watched my phone for updates about the status of my flight, but the application failed to properly alert me. Instead I looked up and suddenly realized that everyone who had been at the gate was no longer there. I ran to the gate and through the door to the jetway, which was still open. As I ran up the jetway to the plane's door, which was also still open, I was intercepted by the gate agent, who sternly told me I had missed the flight and ordered me to go back down the jetway and wait for her there. A few minutes passed, and she finally came back but never addressed me. I finally asked her what could be done to rebook me. She cut me off, telling me she had no time to assist me and that I needed to wait.

So I did. I patiently waited for her to get all of her other issues addressed, when suddenly another male approached her who was quite rude—in stark contrast to the treatment she had been given by me. He spoke to her with the same level of disregard and disrespect she had used in speaking to me. To my dismay, she addressed him and his needs with urgency and courtesy. She even referred to him as a "gentleman," despite his rudeness.

You can well imagine how hurtful that was to me. I was frustrated, and my frustration was trying to turn into unbridled anger. The only difference I could see between me and the other male was that his complexion matched that of the gate agent's, and he was wearing a collared shirt and a blazer. I, on the other hand, was wearing a sweatshirt, sweatpants, and sneakers and my face didn't have their hue. Ironically, I was treating her as a "gentleman" should, and yet she referred to *him* as one—even though he was not "gentle" and certainly not a "*Man*."

After their exchange had ended, I asked her if she now had time to address my needs. She again told me she didn't have time for me and asked her coworker to assist me. Her coworker was also unable to help me. I was stuck in the airport with no resources and no advocacy.

Shortly after that, they began to let people off the flight who did not want to spend the night in the connecting city and rebook them for the following morning. They began to rebook those passengers before they booked me, even though I had been waiting there for almost ninety minutes.

Since they were letting people off the flight, I decided to ask the gate agent if I could board the flight because it appeared that seats might be available. She told me the pilot had said he was not going to allow anyone to board the flight. As luck would have it—or as a *Man* of faith would say, as God would have it—the pilot came off the plane to ask for the new passenger numbers and to get an update on the weather.

Most of the things I heard from the gate agent did not sound or feel right, so I decided to say something to the captain.

"Captain, I sure wish I could board your flight."

He quickly responded, "Well, we're still here!"

To the captain there was no reason I could not board the flight based on its status. I pointed out that I was told I could not board his flight because the gate agent had told me those were his specific orders. He gave the gate agent a look that suggested he had not said that at all. I was in complete shock!

I immediately said to the agent, "You lied!" I pointed out to her that she had treated me terribly and that I was still in limbo after ninety additional minutes of rudeness and constant dismissals. She instructed me to stop or she would call the police. I asked why she would do that, and she simply and earnestly replied, "For public safety."

The irony is that she wanted to call the police "for public safety," which would have put *my* safety at risk. In this day and age, a situation in which the police are called on a black man dressed in a hoodie and sneakers in a secure area of the airport by a white woman with authority, "for public safety" will rarely end well. Fortunately, the captain, knowing that the incident was egregious, came over to apologize to me for her behavior. Their coworker (the other gate agent), who had witnessed everything and eventually rebooked me, thanked me for being so patient and kind. The captain and the other gate agent created a safe space for me just when the situation could have gotten dangerous.

I reported the incident, and the airline officials apologized after a lengthy review of the situation and numerous eyewitness accounts. I have even worked with them since this incident to help ensure that others will not be treated in this manner and explained to them that I believe, as a *Man*, I should not criticize their environment without trying to restore it and elevate it.

Later, when I recounted the incident to friends, they concluded they knew why I was so hurt by the ordeal. They alleged that the gate agent had disregarded my manhood. I could not disagree with them more. My manhood, my life as a servant leader, was intact and not accessible to the agent. *Nothing and nobody can attack my manhood.* The agent didn't disregard my manhood; she disregarded my humanity. What she did was launch an assault—a full-fledged attack—on me as a human being. Very few things on earth are worse than being treated as less than human.

Throughout that ordeal, I could hear the call that all *Men* need to heed: *Create a safe space for those who will come after me, and ensure that I am the tree God intended me to be.*

BE CAREFUL HOW YOU COPE

As the story above illustrates, men are too often exposed to unsafe spaces in our society, particularly men of color. Consequently, providing safety for others in our lives can be challenging because of the constant battle for our own safety. Even *Men* who are wise and mature and who walk in the highest degree of manhood are challenged to remember the mandate of our lives. Even these *Men* can sometimes forget to create safe spaces for others as an act of service, especially when they are routinely under attack and feeling unsafe.

When we continually feel devalued due to these kinds of attacks, we forget just how valuable we are. We can feel beaten down by the pressures of life and the mischaracterizations of some who can only see us as the grown males we used to be. When we find ourselves in this state of confusion and frustration, we can sometimes retreat to our private coping mechanisms.

Unfortunately, some of those coping mechanisms are downright unhealthy, while others are just ill-advised. Some males use their physicality to prey on those who are vulnerable and less fortunate. Others exist in a fit of constant, uncontrollable rage. Some turn to drug and alcohol addiction. And still others attempt to chase away the sorrows of their souls by entertaining multiple women and never settling down with one. The challenge for males, and grown males, whose souls are damaged is that improper coping mechanisms create hostile environments. These damaged souls cause casualties everywhere they go.

I have committed some of these same acts throughout my own life, so I'm certainly not judging anyone. Every *Man* has battles of the flesh that can help him grow and mature when he recognizes them and begins to address them. When we deal with it, we can heal it.

To truly matriculate into the greatest depths of our manhood, we have to swim in the traumas against our humanity.

BE YOUR BROTHER'S KEEPER

My airport story highlights a challenge many men of color face. But we should also understand the issues confronting all men and be prepared to be agents of change and work together to fix problems. We really must be determined to be our brother's keeper and to encourage each other while we fight for change—the kind of change that continually creates safe spaces for those we have been assigned to serve.

No *Man* can run from that assignment, and no male can matriculate into manhood without submitting to its call. There is no higher or more important work for a servant of righteousness than to create safe spaces.

There is no higher or more important work for a servant of righteousness than to create safe spaces.

Adam and Eve managed to rebuild their lives after the fall in the garden. They came together in love and created two bouncing baby boys. Life seemed to be going great. But as the boys began to grow up, they developed two different value systems. The Lord was pleased with Abel, but Cain's anger turned into jealousy, and his jealousy and rejection turned him into a monster. In a fit of rage, he murdered his brother. God, of course, questioned Cain about the missing Abel, and Cain responded sarcastically, "Am I my brother's keeper?" The answer is yes, he was.[1]

As horrible as it sounds, today in America is not that different from the days of Cain. In November 2018, the FBI reported a 17 percent rise in hate crimes. NBC News picked up on the story:

The annual report showed there were 7,175 bias crimes, which targeted 8,493 victims based on their race and sexual orientation, reported in 2017 . . .

164

The hate crime totals were comprised of 59.6 percent acts against a victim based on race, 20.6 percent because of religion and 15.8 percent for sexual orientation, the FBI said.[2]

Furthermore, according to the U.S. Department of Justice (DOJ), "of the 6,370 known offenders, 50.7 percent were white, and 21.3 percent were black or African American ... The race was unknown for 19.1 percent." The DOJ also reported that "of the 4,895 known offenders for whom ages were known, 83.0 percent were 18 years of age or older."[3]

So if we break this down in context, people are being attacked because of the color of their skin, their spiritual or religious beliefs, and their sexual identity. We see that in 50 percent of these crimes, the attacker was white, even though minorities are consistently treated as the more violent of the races. We also see that more than 80 percent of these crimes were committed by people considered legal adults in America. So we cannot dismiss these hate crimes as the work of immature young black and brown teens. These are *grown males* acting out of ignorance and hatred—no more, no less.

A COLLECTIVE EFFORT

What are the *Men* who stand for service, responsibility, and truth to do in a culture where hate crimes are on the rise? How do we educate, inform, and inspire the next generation to make different decisions and reject the intolerances and faulty moral systems of their ancestors?

I'm so glad you asked. We must lead by example and deal with our own prejudices first, and it is going to take all of us—a collective effort—to eradicate the hate. There is only one race—"the human race," as my sister Jane Elliott would say. We are all cousins, distant or not. The minute we get on board with actively focusing on our similarities instead of continually seeking out our differences, we will indeed become one race. Celebrating the ways we are connected while sincerely discussing the ways we are disconnected will bring about the changes we need to see. These are the challenges of today's modern man.

First, we have to start with the fact that *we all need each other* to address the problem of hate adequately—particularly in the area of color or ethnic identity. I am avoiding labeling this an issue of race because, remember, we are supposed to be one race! We need all of our brothers and sisters of all colors. Yes, I said that. Black folks need white folks, and white folks need black folks. And all different colors need one another.

Our white brothers and sisters need to see and acknowledge what is the truth. We all have to come to the consensus that a problem *does exist* and that we all are responsible for our "cousins." Once we acknowledge that we are a family of the same race, it would stand to reason that we should all be fighting *for* each other and not *with* each other. But again, our brothers and sisters who do not share our hue or complexion have to fight for us as we fight for other people.

I am always overjoyed when I see examples like the one that *Fortune* featured in January 2018. They reported that Jessica Chastain, who is white, ensured that she and her costar Octavia Spencer, who is black—both of whom are award-winning actresses—received equal pay for the movie they were working on at that time.[4] As an actor, I was proud, but as a human being, I was over the moon—this is a simple example of people of two colors acting as one race.

That is what it takes. It takes people talking the talk and walking the walk. For instance, when a person of color calls out racism, we should be able to do so without unnecessary persecution. Our voices should be heard on the issue. But we seldom get to do that without immediately being called out as a racist for calling out racism. If we all see each other as the cousins that we are, we will listen to each other with empathetic ears and hearts. When we do that, dramatic transformation happens. Our children witness it, and it teaches them how to right future wrongs while setting a new bar for humanity.

The next area of hatred that needs immediate triage is *religious prejudice*. A young white male (I avoid referencing people by name because I do not wish to attack the person; I am merely attacking *the position* for the sake of transformation) targeted a Charleston, South Carolina, African American church in 2015 and murdered nine people, including a state senator. More recently, eleven people were killed by an older white male in a Pittsburgh, Pennsylvania, synagogue shooting in October 2018. Nationally, more than half of all religious hate crimes are committed against persons who follow the Jewish religion, according to the 2017 report released by the FBI.[5] The FBI also reported that Wisconsin's religious crimes went from eight in 2016 to seventeen in 2017, which is more than a 50 percent increase in a year.[6]

It seems as if we're in a time when hatred and intolerance have become something that gives people the right to act on their fears. Disdain is fueling violence. As a society, we must become more conscious of the things that can cause us to lose perspective and that activate our flesh in violent ways. We are not spending enough time examining ourselves and our lives. Past pain, trauma, and other negative experiences serve as the propellant for acts that cause great devastation to ourselves and others. Religious hatred is something we all must earnestly protest—whether or not we agree with different religions and their doctrines. We must teach our children that this kind of bias, as well as all other biases, is just wrong.

My spirituality is directed by the information, instruction, and guidance I get from the Bible. How I live my life is based on the direction I get from the Word. I use the Word as my life's blueprint, and I use my peers—other great *Men*—as my earthly accountability whenever I'm confused about how to use Christ as my model for manhood.

No matter what anyone says, you do not need a physical building or the structure of a religion to be a godly *Man* or a *Man* of righteousness. Church and religion were meant to provide earthly accountability for humankind. However, with all the misguidedness and misdirection, and sometimes abuse, that many people have experienced in the church, some have been turned off by the thought of religion and are reluctant to find their way back.

While we work on building good church homes, of which there are still many, we should make sure we serve as the pastor of our families and community circles.

ABOUT SEXUALITY

Back in 1991, the hip-hop trio Salt-N-Pepa released a single titled "Let's Talk about Sex." And that's what we need to do right now— have a real-deal, no-joke discussion about sexual identity in the United States. We must understand that no matter what we believe spiritually, no matter what color we are, we all have people in our communities who are battling with their sexual identity. We cannot just pretend that only heterosexual human beings walk the face of the earth. It's time to address this issue in the way we are being called to. When we've dealt with it before, we've left a lot of people hurt and damaged. Let's not do that again. I believe we are being called to engage with people without judgment, but with a spirit and a heart that can properly assess what needs to be done that is righteous and will bridge a gap for our brothers and sisters.

If we lovingly respond to our LGBTQ family, we will have less suicide, less depression, and ultimately less retreating behavior from that community because they feel shamed and unsupported.[7] We will have fewer males and females living "in the closet" and having secret relationships "on the down low" because they are not free to be themselves. We will have fewer people getting married to the opposite sex because they feel like they need to assimilate and have children to validate their existence in the "straight" world, only to leave their families because the burden of the secret they've been carrying is too much to bear. We will have fewer people "tricking" people or not being completely honest with their potential partners about how they transitioned to their new sexual identity.

Society's definition of the word *man* suggests he should be categorized as such based on his sexual orientation—based on whether he has sex with a woman. For far too long we have accepted this rudimentary, spiritually lacking definition of what a *Man* is. Not only is it outdated, but it lacks truth at its core. We all know of a great many males who have had sex with a great many women. They have likewise biologically "fathered" many children and simultaneously left all of them uncovered. Is *that* a *Man*? No. Why do we choose to neglect the true definition of a *Man*—what it means to be a *Man* rather than a child? Being a *Man* is not based on our physicality or our sexuality, but is in fact based on our *commitment to service*. That definition sounds just like what I have been describing in this book. A *Man* is a male who is dedicated to *being of service*, in contrast to a child, who is a male dedicated to *being served*. This means that a homosexual or gay brother may fall under the descriptive umbrella of what a *Man* is.

The truth is, I know some trifling heterosexual males and I know some trifling homosexual males, but at the same time, I also know amazing and honorable *Men* who are heterosexual and those who are homosexual. I know some who are bisexual and—you guessed it—transsexual as well.

I can hear the many judgmental voices out there right now screaming, "How can you say that? Do you not know what the Bible says?" Yes, I do! Remember, I am not a judge. That's not my job or intention. I am a servant, and as such, my job is to give my people what they need to righteously walk out the essence of being a *Man*—authenticity, clarity, and empathy. Shaming our brothers and sisters for who they are and what they identify as will not bridge the gaps of our humanity. When these brothers and sisters are forced to hide in shame, our society is robbed of all that we can receive from them. We must restore our brothers and sisters in the LGBTQ community to their rightful and dignified place in our culture and in God's story for all of his children.

We live in a time when our brothers and sisters who identify as something other than the gender they were born into are now able to go to the restroom of their choice. These types of scenarios are not going away. Nor should they have to. Ever! We cannot continue to address new issues with old ideals. It is one of the reasons we are stuck in so many areas of life as a people and have a society that lacks civility.

As a righteous people, God's people, we lack empathy and understanding when we so often stand in judgment. I have seen so many of our church families hold a space of judgment, being entirely unwilling to address the issues due to fear. And then we sometimes use Scripture as the reason for refusing to love others or make a place for our brothers and sisters. The argument has been, "Well, if homosexuality were righteous, homosexuals would be able to procreate." We all know the arguments, and we also know what the Word says. What I also know is that none of those things are enough to get me to shut out any of my brothers and sisters from feeling God's love. Period!

We must restore our brothers and sisters in the LGBTQ community to their rightful and dignified place in our culture and in God's story for all of his children.

The church was never meant to be a place of judgment. Because people are communal, the church was intended as a space of fellowship. It was meant to provide us with structure and, of course, to be a loving space of accountability in the ways of Jesus Christ. Christ did a great many things with a great many types of people. He showed understanding and not judgment and delivered God's message and his undying love. We have failed miserably in speaking a message of love to our LGBTQ family and providing them a seat at the table with us. As a singular race of people, we allow so many things to divide us. As *Men*, we are called to find the things that will instead unite us.

We are called to measure *Men* by their actions, the content of their character, and the service they provide to their families and communities and to be less concerned about others' sexual orientation. It sometimes feels like we are afraid to sit with these brothers, as if something is going to rub off on us or that sitting with them may reveal something about us. It sometimes seems like we give the impression that we think we are the better version of *Man* just because of our sexuality. We are mixing up our sexuality with our manhood. One refers to our sexual preference, while the other refers to our dedication to service.

The days of allowing judgment and arrogance to serve as the master version of manhood must be put behind us. These kinds of prejudices are extremely dangerous, as are all prejudices, and they prevent us from hearing the call to be the *Men* God created to mirror Christ.

I recently watched a documentary about children groomed at the hands of adult sexual predators. I witnessed the accounts of two abused men who later became husbands and fathers. What amazed me was how these men had allowed themselves to speak their truth about their sexual assaults and refused to let the shame of their experiences prevent them from releasing the toxins of their secrets. They happened to be white men who had been molested as young children at the hands of an extremely powerful and influential male whom they, as well as their parents, idolized!

I thought to myself, *Wow, it must be empowering to be able to speak your truth and not have your community shame you for something you could not control as a child.* It spoke so loudly because many black men sometimes feel so judged by our community and so shunned by the church (unless, of course, we're talking about the choir director) that they never feel as if they can take their rightful place in either space. I have spoken to many *Men* who happen to be gay, and we've had candid conversations about their sexuality. I do this because I am always seeking a greater understanding and awareness of our gender and humanity. Once I know that they understand my heart and my intentions, I ask this question: "How did you arrive at your sexuality?" Some say it is a chemical thing, like through DNA; some say it is experiential, like a safely curious exploration or a devastatingly irreversible molestation.

I firmly believe our sexual experience isn't necessarily the exercise of our sexuality. Just because someone experienced sexual abuse at the hands of someone of the same sex, it does not make that person homosexual; it only makes him someone who had an encounter with someone who molested him, and they just happened to be the same sex. For instance—and this is a painful and extreme example, but I have to drive this home with proper context—if a girl is molested by a straight male, it does not make her a straight male; it makes her a victim of sexual assault. So, in turn, if a male is molested by another male, it does not make him a homosexual or a sexual predator; it makes him a victim of sexual assault.

I have heard so many of my brothers express how confusing it was to come back to feeling heterosexual after feeling aroused during these kinds of attacks that society would label as homosexual. In my opinion, we must reclassify these attacks. They should be categorized as molestations and nothing more. To call them homosexual experiences is to redefine who someone could be and could *shame* them into feeling they have to keep that label. It can be quite confusing to many of us because when we hear that a sexual assault left the victim feeling any pleasure at all, we ignorantly think it must mean they were complicit and that the sexual experience was an exercise of their sexuality. It was not.

After having this discussion with one of my gay brothers, he said to me, "Dondré, I always said to myself, *How can I see myself as straight once I've had a penis in my mouth?*" It was one of the most profound exchanges I have ever had in my life! I cried for, and with, my brother, and I hugged him—*Man* to *Man*, brother to brother, servant to servant.

When we shame people, we send them into a state of retreat, causing them to isolate themselves because the shame is too much to handle. When this occurs, it can make people stay "in the closet" or even have relationships on the down low. Those experiences are about secrets, and those secrets are about retreating. Retreating allows them to avoid the shame that comes with so many of those secrets.

To deal honestly with the challenges facing today's modern man, we have to acknowledge that there are different types of men. *Men* are not monolithic, but *manhood* is. Manhood is based on service, truth, and responsibility—*not* on sexual orientation, masculinity, or physical strength. I know some sexually impotent *Men*. I know some *Men* who have high voices. I know some who do not wear boots, jeans, and hoodies, and I know some who cannot bench-press 150 pounds, yet all of them are *Men* who serve with responsibility and truth.

CHAPTER 10

CHANGE VS. HEALING:

Hitting the Reset Button

I am always blown away by the reactions of perpetrators who get caught in an act of wrongdoing. In our 24/7–news cycle, meme-creating culture, their reactions are hard to miss.

When the person begins to express an apology, I am intrigued and often wonder, *How does this person hit the reset button? How do they come to a space of change, and can they achieve that without mending what has been fractured? And what is the percentage of people who are genuinely sorry for their actions versus those who are just sorry they got caught?*

Maybe it's just me, and I won't call out any names, but I am astounded by people who victimize others for decades and then want to claim "victim status" themselves once they are exposed. Involuntary exposure is the worst way to come clean to moral failings. And I believe a *Man* does not take any pleasure in witnessing a fellow brother or sister give an account in public for private sins. Instead, a *Man* desires that every person would repent before they are exposed because exposure does not just affect the perpetrator; their victims are also exposed and forced to recall all of the horrid details of every unjust action that was done to them. So in a perfect world, every person committing sins and transgressions would become whole and healed and stop their misdeeds before they are revealed to the public.

> *Males create hurting cultures, while* Men *create healing cultures.*

We need to become a healing culture. As we've already said, a *Man* has to pride himself on being first and in so doing become a catalyst for change and healing. Males create hurting cultures, while *Men* create healing cultures.

THE IMPORTANCE
OF REPENTANCE

So here is the question: What does a healing culture look like? Well, the first step to establishing a healing culture starts with one word: *repentance*. Because I am a follower of Christ, I identify with spiritual people. But I am not what I call a "religious person" who believes in merely giving lip service to the words in the Good Book but never has any intentions of carrying out the commandments as they were given. The difference between a follower of Christ and a "religious" person can be clearly seen in how they repent.

A portion of my family is from the Bible Belt. They have taught me that repentance is not merely an act but a series of actions. If friends or relatives got in trouble in a "religious" family, it basically took a modern-day exorcism for the "sinner" to get delivered. I mean, they had to speak in tongues and go to an all-night prayer service. I also have not-so-great, vivid memories of people (mainly pregnant, unwed mothers) who had to stand in front of the church and ask the church folk to forgive them of their sins. While I am an actor, I am not describing something from a script; I am describing something that takes place in the lives of plenty of normal, everyday folks.

I don't want to knock anyone's belief system, but I would be remiss if I did not state clearly that repentance has very little to

178

do with anything we *say*; it has far more to do with what we *do*. Repentance requires two things: a change of your mind and a change of your heart.

Another way of saying it is this: we have to let our mind believe and allow our heart to receive.

The two elements of repentance are the doorway to renewal of your mental, emotional, psychological, and spiritual health. Repentance of the mind leads to renewal of the heart, but you cannot renew your heart until the changing of your mind has taken place. People often get this concept confused. Some of us think our heart changes and then our mind follows. Yet nothing can change the heart until the mind is changed. People act on what they feel in their heart. Often people are encouraged to "say what is on your heart." Well, I submit to you that nothing on your heart is ever changed until you change what is in your mind. Whatever is in your mind will soon be on your heart.

This process is hugely successful in spurring people to act righteously. And it helps people know what to be repentant about. We first have to understand the state of our spirituality. We have to continually check ourselves in order to determine what we need to supplement our spirituality—a change of our mind and a change of our heart. Self-examination is critical in order to achieve transformation. And that transformation is vital for us to become the best version of the *Man* we intend to be.

Unfortunately, many of us never experience significant change because we are unwilling to go through significant self-examination. One of the differentiations between *Men* and grown males is that *Men* are always examining themselves. They consistently reflect on their words and deeds to be sure they are living out their lives in a way that serves others and not merely themselves.

Accountability to others is a powerful necessity for a *Man*, but accountability *to himself* through self-examination is the most powerful part of his manhood process. For example, at the end of each day, I examine my words and deeds by sitting alone in a quiet space where I can meditate on the experiences of my day. This is the equivalent of what an athlete does in a "film session" to dissect their on-field or on-court performance. Without making this commitment, an athlete never gets to become a better version of themselves. This is where they play back the good, the bad, and the ugly of their execution so they can better execute in the future. Avoiding the examination of self and the assessment of how we perform when we experience pressure situations keeps us from growing as a *Man*.

> *Accountability to others is a powerful necessity for a* Man, *but accountability to himself is the most powerful part of his manhood process.*

Taking time for reflection will help us make sure we are executing a life of service rather than a life of gathering insubstantial things that gratify our flesh. We will always be tempted by our flesh. But the temptation is not the sin; giving in to the temptation is! Living a life of repentance is extremely important, and it is impossible to achieve without self-examination.

READING THE BIBLE

Life presents us with a constant series of tests. One of the verses that gives guidance for facing life's trials is 2 Timothy 3:16: "All Scripture is God-breathed and is useful for teaching, rebuking, correcting and training in righteousness."

I want to zero in on that last phrase—"training in righteousness" —because it says to me that God knew we would need tools to assist with self-examination and that we would need a playbook to operate from. God left his Word as a means for us to train in righteousness and to have the righteous plays we need to execute as we pursue a life of manhood.

I often speak to *Men* who express that they are not interested in "getting biblical." And I always respond, "Good. Me either!" I want to get righteous. I want to have a road map to get there. The Bible has become my navigation system to help me make my way through these challenging times. It helps me be the *Man* I am called to be. Even if I were not as spiritual as I am and wanted to get some messaging that helps me live a great life, I could go to the book of Proverbs, which has so many gems that are the absolute keys to our manhood. I tell anyone who will listen that I have applied so many biblical teachings to every facet of my life. It gives me so much clarity and counsels me in every area of life. It is a one-stop shop for me! And if I do my part and train myself according to what the Word says, I will lead a great life.

Think of it this way. When we train our bodies, we are usually in the gym to focus on certain parts of the body that need to become stronger. Well, I often say that when life continues to hit me in a specific area, it usually means I need repetitions in that particular realm of my life. We do not get strong in the gym by doing a couple of reps and then rushing off to the next exercise. That's just not how building dense and functional muscle works. Typically, we are doing reps on that one machine or for that one exercise, and the reps that count are the ones we do when we think we have nothing left in our tank—to exhaustion. We may do multiple sets of double-digit push-ups, and at first we may feel as if we are going to die, but eventually we grow strong from the consistent repetitions—so much so that we can't imagine going back to a time when we were weak and couldn't do twenty, fifty, or a hundred solid push-ups. We are training our bodies to endure, and in the same way we teach our bodies, we have to train our spirits. The process of training our spirits is the process of repentance. When we do, we experience a renewal of our minds, which leads to a renewal of our hearts.

The process of training our spirits is the process of repentance. When we do, we experience a renewal of our minds, which leads to a renewal of our hearts.

The apostle Paul says it this way in Romans 12:2 (ESV): "Do not be conformed to this world, but be transformed by the renewal of your mind, that by testing you may discern what is the will of God, what is good and acceptable and perfect."

Renewing anything means that somewhere along the line, we have some outdated software in our system. To renew this outdated software, we should uncover the areas we are hurting in and the areas of trauma that cause so much pain. At some point, we all have to deal with the pain of our past. We are called to deal with the things that hurt us.

Who left you?

Who did you let stay too long?

Who abused you?

Who discouraged you?

These and every other trauma you have faced have led you to become a fraction of what God intended you to be. In the end, to get to a better version of ourselves, to renew ourselves, we are called to put in some intensely diligent work.

However, because we have been created in the image of God,

we have some supernatural powers we can tap into that will help us, heal us, and transform us into the whole beings God intended us to be. This repentance and renewal process does not always allow us to see an outward change immediately, but it is significant just the same. In fact, the process creates levels of change in our personality, character, and emotional perspective. The *internal* change is the thing that influences the *external* change. The internal change, which takes place through our repentance, is the thing *we* experience, and the external change—the transformation—is what *others* experience. The apostle Paul describes it this way:

> Brothers and sisters, I could not address you as people who live by the Spirit but as people who are still worldly—mere infants in Christ. I gave you milk, not solid food, for you were not yet ready for it. Indeed, you are still not ready. You are still worldly. For since there is jealousy and quarreling among you, are you not worldly? Are you not acting like mere humans? For when one says, "I follow Paul," and another, "I follow Apollos," are you not mere human beings?
>
> What, after all, is Apollos? And what is Paul? Only servants, through whom you came to believe—as the Lord has assigned to each his task. I planted the seed, Apollos watered it, but God has been making it grow. So neither the one who plants nor the one who waters is anything, but only God, who makes things grow.[1]

At the beginning of our process, we cannot handle the meaty or weighty things of life. That is just another element that separates *Men* from grown males. *Men* grow, change, and transform; they put away petty arguing, as this passage suggests.

Change comes to form the spaces in us where we actively heal. I let the Spirit into those places. I ask God to help me heal. When we hit the reset button, we are allowing ourselves to put into motion the necessary renewal that comes through repentance.

We *Men* have more important things to do than chase our fleshly appetites. Males do that. We *Men* each have assigned tasks to do and must remain busy fulfilling them. This fulfillment can come only from a state of renewal and repentance. If we honestly expect to be more whole, then we have to hit the necessary reset buttons that prepare us for transformation.

You were made in God's image. Just imagine you are a soldier—in fact, an officer of righteousness—who has been commissioned to go out and cover your troops, God's people. He has put that purpose on our lives. My brothers, *let's do this*!

CHAPTER 11

"THAT HIT THE SPOT"

Wait, hear me out! Before you think you have arrived at the cafeteria of *Man* U, let me assure you that while this chapter is about food, it's not about the kind you eat. This is the kind of food that feeds our spirits, edifies us, and helps us grow as godly *Men*. When a *Man* says, *"That* hit the spot," he's generally indicating that what he just consumed was good—so good that it satisfied his appetite and exceeded his expectations, thus allowing him to have a sense of calm and peace.

This chapter is about the role that God must play in my life in order for me to remain in a state of humility and service that will usher me into a similar sense of calm and peace, though to a much greater degree than what food can provide. God is truly one of the biggest keys to our sustained walk as *Men*. His love and Christ's example of service should be what we hunger for. Honoring him will leave us spiritually satiated in much the same way that plant-based foods affect our bodies and satisfy our appetites due to their nutrient-dense content.

SUPERNATURAL STRENGTH AND POWER

I have been a vegan now for three years, and it has been very good to and for me. It has profoundly changed my health, specifically with regard to inflammation and chronic pain. I used to experience pain in my left knee when I was eating a diet rich in meats and dairy. I thought the chronic pain was just the result of getting older. However, after I committed to eating strictly plant-based foods, the pain went away almost immediately. The only thing that changed in my lifestyle was my diet. It wasn't easy or convenient, but it was well worth it. I literally changed nothing but my diet, and my body has responded.

The minute we commit to change is usually the minute we experience growth. When something in life isn't growing the way we want it to, we have to change something about its circumstances in order to kick-start growth. Allowing the circumstances to remain the same produces the same result. That's why doing the same thing over and over again while expecting different results is said to be the definition of insanity.

Now again, I'm not telling you that being a vegan is the only way to live a healthy lifestyle. I'm telling you that it's an *effective* way to do so. Additionally, I'm not telling you that there is only one path to seeking a righteous lifestyle. But uncovering God's will for your life and having a consistent diet of instruction from the Bible are *effective* ways to do so. As *Men*, we must constantly seek ways to grow beyond our current existence and boost our upward trajectory. This will feed our appetite to be the servant leaders God has ordained us to be. Moreover, we have to be intentional about pursuing our mental, psychological, and emotional fitness. Ensuring that these areas are cared for properly allows us to focus on our spiritual center—a spiritual center that has been created to be fed only by God Almighty.

There is no way I could do any of the things I do well, with any level of consistency, without a supernatural source of strength and power to draw upon.

If we are going to access a great life, we should first acknowl-edge the importance of the spot that God can fill for all of us. One of the ways we gain access is through our relationship with him. We have to be diligent about our relationship because it is the source of righteous power we need to remain in alignment with his purpose for our lives. God is the power source that keeps me fully charged and ready to walk out my intended life. Again, the key is my relationship and sub-mitting to a higher power that keeps me grounded.

When our mental, psychological, and emotional fitness is cared for properly, it allows us to focus on our spiritual center.

I work with many people, and I'm closer to some of them than others. I often say, "My network is vast, but my circle is small." This is the way it should be. Not everyone is meant to have access to you at all times. Only the people in my inner circle can call me or have extensive text conversations with me. The people beyond my circle must arrange a time for us to connect when it is appropriate, and the same is probably true for you.

For instance, have you ever had a good friend change their phone number? When they call, you may not pick up, even though they have a relationship with you. But because they cannot be properly identified due to their new phone number, their access to you is temporarily denied. That's what happens when we decide we want to live without a relationship with God. This is the way relationships work. We temporarily lose access because we did not do what was necessary to maintain a proper line of commu-nication. In fact, we have not worked hard enough to maintain a proper relationship.

Now, of course, we know God is still there. The Word says he will never leave us or forsake us.[1] However, we do not have the same benefits and blessings as our brothers and sisters who stay in relationship and are truly connected to our source of life. I want to help each one of us get back to having a proper line of communication with God so we can access the abundance of life from the generator of life.

HOW TO KEEP YOUR RELATIONSHIP WITH GOD STRONG

First, we must have a healthy fear of the Lord and his commandments. All children should be mindful of their parents' rules and mandates on their lives. Refusing to submit to the rules set by the parents can prevent the child from gaining the intended access to their parents' house. In our case, when we do not abide by the rules of our heavenly Father, we miss out on the directions for life, the blessings for our lives, and the inheritance of our Father's house.[2] We should always want to obey him because we know that obedience is the pathway to all things with God. Think of it this way. Have you ever had a child who did not obey you? If so, you probably did not feel very loved, respected, or appreciated by that child. Think about how God feels when we do not submit to him. Remember, to submit does not mean to quit. To quit means to give up; to submit means to give over!

I believe many of us struggle with our heavenly Father because we struggle with our earthly fathers. If we have experienced any fractures in our relationships with our biological fathers, we are likely to struggle with obedience to our heavenly Father. When you think about it along these lines, it's easy to empathize when someone struggles in their relationship with God. I struggled mightily with my biological father—struggling to trust him, to love him, and most of all to have faith in him because I never had him show up for me in a tangible and significant way. You can clearly see how my struggles with God—the Father I cannot see—stemmed from the conflicts I had with the father I could see, if he had decided to *make himself seen.*

The good news is that God is no ordinary parent, and as a result, we do not have to settle for ordinary lives. The way out of my ordinary life was an *extraordinary* connection with God. To gain access to that kind of relationship, I had to invest in it in the same way I look to foster other great relationships. We should always be diligent, transparent, giving, and unselfish.

Next, God requires us to have honesty. Whether you spend time in quiet meditation or self-examination, or if you are someone who struggles with praying regularly, I would encourage you to have more "talks" with God. Many of us think that prayer is some overly poetic, holier-than-thou, ready-to-be-published communication with God—and that couldn't be further from the truth. *Prayer is merely an honest connection and communication with our Father.* Even if we are not feeling very connected to him, all he requires is that we communicate with honesty. Our responsibility is to keep the line of communication open. This will allow us to gain access to him and have our calls identified. Have an honest conversation out loud with him as if he were right beside you. That's all that prayer is—an open dialogue with the one who gave you life and gives you provision.

I'm certain some brothers are asking, "How does this help me in my life as a *Man*?" Well, if you practice having honest conversations and communication with God, and if you speak respectfully and righteously to him, then you will become qualified to do so with your spouse, your children, and your community at large. All of the ways we practice a healthy relationship with God are the same ways we practice healthy relationships with those in our lives. Maybe as a loving parent, God knew how important our communication with him would be for all the other connections in our lives. And I am certain he loved us so much that he made the connection with him *necessary* for those reasons.

THE IMAGE OF GOD

Furthermore, a powerful level of communication with God helps us have a deeper understanding of ourselves. After all, we are created in the image of God, so having a deeper relationship with him helps us understand *who and what we need to be* in our lives for the sake of others.

Let's take this a step further. Our relationships with our significant others will not work without honesty. This is also true of our relationship with God. What is funny is that the things we try to keep from God are nonsensical, because God says in Isaiah 46:10, "I make known the end from the beginning," and Revelation 22:13 says that Christ is "the Alpha and the Omega, the First and the Last, the Beginning and the End."

So transparency can be freeing for us. God already knows everything about our lives. But what he wants is our communication with him. This is similar to a relationship with a spouse, a friend, or a relative. At some point, after you spend a significant amount of time with them, they know you almost better than you know yourself.

I always chuckle at guys I see in restaurants who have clearly been married for a long time. It seems at times that they don't even know what to order from the menu! It's great when their spouse, due to a strong connection, comes to their aid and orders for them because they know their spouse's appetites! In a much more profound way, of course, God knows our appetites too. He knows our good appetites as well as the ones we struggle with in our flesh. That is why it is so important to communicate with him about our struggles. It helps us express those same kinds of things to our loving accountability partners here on earth.

THE MOST IMPORTANT COMMANDMENT

A healthy relationship with God will also affect the way you view people. You cannot love God and not love other people.

> One of the teachers of the law came and heard them debating. Noticing that Jesus had given them a good answer, he asked him, "Of all the commandments, which is the most important?"
>
> "*The most important one*," answered Jesus, "*is this*: 'Hear, O Israel: The Lord our God, the Lord is one. Love the Lord your God with all your heart and with all your soul and with all your mind and with all your strength.' The second is this: 'Love your neighbor as yourself.' There is no commandment greater than these."
>
> "Well said, teacher," the man replied. "You are right in saying that God is one and there is no other but him. To love

him with all your heart, with all your understanding and with all your strength, and to love your neighbor as yourself is more important than all burnt offerings and sacrifices."[3]

And 1 John 4:20–21 (MSG) says, "If anyone boasts, 'I love God,' and goes right on hating his brother or sister, thinking nothing of it, he is a liar. If he won't love the person he can see, how can he love the God he can't see? The command we have from Christ is blunt: Loving God includes loving people. You've got to love both."

Life requires loving both God and people. When we do that, we set ourselves up for the good life that hits the spot. Though we know life is not always easy, it is much easier because of our relationship with the Father. When we walk with God, we witness how he intercedes on behalf of all of us. We cannot go right on hating our brother and sister.

I have a ten-year-old son, and it is incredible how much he is like me. Yet it makes perfect sense. Not only is he made in my image—he looks just like I did when I was his age—but because of our *relationship* (there's that word again), he acts as I would in many instances. He is the kind of giving soul who will intercede on behalf of others, particularly when he sees that someone needs empathy and assistance. He is already a great servant. And again, he has adopted that way because I have modeled this way for him to mirror. Now, as similar as he is to his father in those ways, there are times he will act out of his flesh and go against my teachings. And just as God does for me and all of us, I have to intercede on his behalf when I know he is about to go the wrong way in life. My son pretty much lives a life of service to others. I have been doing my best to model for him what has been modeled for me by God. It is uncanny how all of this works together for our good.

We must be reminded continually that there is someone higher than us—and for me that is God. Why is that so important to remember? Because when we think we are the highest, we can easily slip into a state of feeling we should be served. We stop acting like *Men* and revert back to acting like grown males.

When we know God is higher, it immediately reminds us that we should be *humble servants*. This call to servanthood will often get lost when we lose sight of the fact that there is a divine order. If we are the head, then we get put into the position of the one who should be served. But when we put God at the head, we are activated to serve him and to serve his children on his behalf. It may sound like a simple concept, but I promise you that this one is key to faithfully living a righteous life.

Know this: God did not create us with the intention of withholding our happiness until our lives on earth are done. He very much intended us to be happy here on this earth. He did not send us here as a form of punishment or because he did not love us. We wish for all those we love to have health, wholeness, and prosperity. Well, if God intended us to be happy, why are so many of us unhappy? Unhappiness becomes more frequent the farther we get from our source.

Think of it like having a cell phone and getting too far from the signal tower. The voice on the line will go in and out, and eventually you will lose your connection altogether. It is not until you get closer to the signal tower that you regain a connection. God is the signal tower that allows us to have clarity. He provides it to us, even when we are in a space that feels barren or remote.

Years ago, while I was between acting jobs, I had to get another job to supplement my income. I began loading trucks for a huge shipping company during what they call "peak season"—Christmastime.

Many nights, well past the midnight hour, I worked in that hub loading two and a half 18-wheelers by myself. It was freezing cold inside, but I was sweating profusely from the amount of energy I had to exert to keep up with the constant deluge of packages. I had to read the packages first in order to know whether they belonged in that load, and then I had to build a wall with those packages to prevent them from sliding everywhere during transport. The work was relentless, so whenever I felt weak, I prayed.

From time to time, just to make sure we were reading the packages properly, a supervisor would purposely throw a "bomb" (a package that didn't belong in our load) onto our loading belt. If you did not catch that "bomb," you had to break your wall, find it in order to retrieve it for the supervisor, and then rebuild your wall again.

It was excruciating, backbreaking work, and I hated it. So I prayed. Every night I had to walk home because I had no car! In the freezing, snow-driven cold, I would walk, feeling the loneliness of the world. This time was isolating and barren. So I prayed. When I got to my unfurnished apartment, I would take a shower and sit on the mattress situated on the floor as exhausted tears streamed steadily down my face. The most I had ever made in a week on that job was $150. And whenever rent was due, I had no idea how I was going to pay it. So I prayed. Miraculously, I would always seem to get a residual check from another job I had done on television that then aired as a rerun. It happened so many times that I cannot even give you a guess as to just how many.

God was showing up so mightily. He was sending me signals that I was not alone, that even in my darkest, most barren times he was there. A couple of months later, I landed a multiyear contract on *All My Children* opposite my buddy Kelly Ripa, and the rest, as they say, is history.

I prayed during those times to maintain my connection with God. As long as we have our connection, the clarity about our lives will always exist. But the further we get from our connection with God, the murkier the vision for our life will be. Make the proper adjustments to stay in connection with him. Pray. Read the Word. Meditate and do self-reflection. The state of our lives will mirror the state of our connection with God.

Finding the good spot in life is being in connection, in relationship, with the Spirit of God. We are the sum total of our connection with him, and

It is our job to rebrand what a Man is by modeling it for the world daily.

so we should be diligent about seeking him so we can find our purpose and be fulfilled as *Men*—the humble servants he has sent for this day, for such a time as this!

As I mentioned previously, males have damaged our brand—the brand of *Man*. They have done so by rebuking righteousness. It is our job to rebrand what a *Man* is by modeling it for the world daily. Eventually the world will begin to mirror who *we* are. Let's be diligent in our intention and walk out our purpose of service that has been mandated.

The call to action is this—our job is to let the world see who we are based on our service. Let's resuscitate our family and community by being what we were designed to be—a *Man*!

ACKNOWLEDGMENTS

I dedicate this book to every woman who doesn't have a *Man* who covers them the way God intentioned us to be their covering. When I speak to women, I see them through the filter of women most important to me—my grandmother, mother, wife, and daughter.

In that vein, I give thanks:

- to my grandmother, Callie Mae Whitfield (may she rest in peace), who taught me to be a maverick.
- to my mother, Vonda Bembry, who gave me the vital building blocks I have built my manhood on.
- to my wife, Salli Richardson Whitfield, who stretched me, doubted me (which served me in a godly way), and fought *for* me more than she fought *with* me.
- to my daughter, Parker Whitfield, whose life activated me to be even more of a *Man* the minute she was born.

Thanks also go out:

- to my bonus moms—Marcia Harris, who has shown me her love through her trust, and Sandy Peppers, who treated me like a son even in the midst of losing her own.
- to my sisters, Traci Blackwell, who probably has spoken more confirmation over my life than any woman I know, and Halle Berry, who, in my service to her, gave me sisterhood, love, and trust that would propel my purpose work.
- to Nicole Beharie, Tisha Campbell Martin, and Jennifer Freeman—and all of the countless sisters who were assigned to me to serve. I thank you all for your faith and confidence.
- lastly to Ms. Patti LaBelle, who taught me that I should do what I'm passionate about as if my life depended on it.

I further dedicate this book to every *Man* who has ever spoken words of wisdom into my life—who helped shape me into the *Man* I am and inspired me to elevate my manhood. I often say you don't need to be fathered by your biological dad, but you do need to be fathered.

In that vein, I give thanks:

- to my stepfather, James Bembry, who was the first example in my life of how a *Man* could take someone else's child and help cover them.
- to my grandfather, John Henry Whitfield (they don't even make John Henrys anymore)—may he rest in peace—who taught me unwavering strength.
- to my brothers, Jaimey Bembry, who inspires me to keep growing and never allow people to put me in a box, and

Davon Bembry, who is always an example that laughter is extremely important in life (just not as much as he thinks).

- to both of my bonus dads—Leroy Harris (may he rest in peace), who taught me to investigate life and to speak the truth, and Duel Richardson, who modeled for me that I need to lean more on my mentality and less on my physicality.

Thanks also go out:

- to Conrad Johns, who served as a great example of calm and clarity.
- to Anthony Abeson, my first acting teacher at Performing Arts High School (LaGuardia), who showed me colorless love when color was my major obstacle in life.
- to my friend Matt Fisher, who used golf as a distraction in order to sneak God's messaging into me.
- to my best friend, Hasani Pettiford, who God sent as a conduit to alert me of my purpose and my gift as a messenger and who helps increase me as a *Man*.
- to my additional best friend, Erin Jones, who came into my life to give me balance and to remind me of the notion that we live by daily "why not?"

I want to express my deep gratitude as well:

- to Muhammad Ali, who taught me how to be a *Man* who doesn't allow worldly possessions to compromise his manhood.
- to my deceased best friend, Amon Parker (who my daughter is named after), whose loss reminds me of what can happen

to a *Man* when he doesn't stand his post. Amon, I will never make the mistake again! I honor you with this work.

• to Jesus Christ, whose life on this earth was the model I mirror and the One I honor daily with the service of my life.

Okay, two last "finallys." First, to my biological father—I give you the grace that God gives us every day, and I'm sorry you didn't get what you needed in order for you to be what you needed for yourself and to be what I needed. And second, I dedicate this book with thanksgiving to my son, my twin—Dré Whitfield. I was once asked who I would be if I could be someone else. Without hesitation, I said, "My son!" I've always had great potential in life but few resources—not to mention the absence of my father who would guide my steps in the ways of manhood every day.

My son has what I always wanted—great potential, endless resources, and a father whose assignment is to grow him into the *Man* that God intentioned to serve the world. Son, may this book be a constant component of growth in your manhood journey.

NOTES

Prerequisite
1. John 6:63.
2. Romans 8:5–6.

Chapter 1: What Is a *Man*?
1. See Philippians 2:5–11.
2. Read Genesis 3 for the whole story.
3. The phrase "weaker vessel" comes from 1 Peter 3:7 in the classic translation of the Bible, the King James Version, as well as in a few other modern translations. You won't actually see it in the Adam and Eve story in Genesis.
4. 1 Corinthians 13:11.
5. Another phrase from the Bible—Proverbs 27:17.
6. Romans 6:6 ESV.
7. Maya Angelou, Twitter post, August 12, 2018, 8:23 a.m., https://twitter.com/drmayaangelou/status/1028663286512930817.
8. Read Genesis 1 and 2. We are made "in the image of God."

Chapter 2: What Is a Male?
1. Thorgil Bjornson, "It's Okay to Be Male: Masculinity in Crisis on International Male Day," November 19, 2018, https://medium

.com/@thorgilbjornson/its-okay-to-be-male-f782c8213250, italics original.

2. Maasai Warriors, "Facing the Lion," Maasai Association, www .maasai-association.org/lion.html.
3. "Failure to Thrive," Children's Hospital of Philadelphia, www .chop.edu/conditions-diseases/failure-thrive.
4. Richard Fry, "For First Time in Modern Era, Living with Parents Edges Out Other Living Arrangements for 18–34-Year-Olds," Pew Research Center, May 24, 2016, www.pewsocialtrends.org /2016/05/24/for-first-time-in-modern-era-living-with-parents -edges-out-other-living-arrangements-for-18-to-34-year-olds.
5. Patrick Sisson, "Millennials: The Savvy, Stay-at-Home Generation: Data Shows Millennials Are Living at Home with Their Parents in Record Numbers," *Curbed*, October 10, 2017, www.curbed.com/2017/10/10/16450394/millennial-living-at -home-housing-homeownership.

Chapter 3: Calm in Chaos

1. See 1 Samuel 17.
2. Read Genesis 1:26–28.
3. Matthew 19:26.
4. 1 John 4:4.
5. James 2:26 NKJV.

Chapter 4: Healing for Where It Hurts

1. Michelle Obama, *Becoming* (New York: Crown, 2018).
2. Read Genesis 1 and 2 again. God created people to be in community with each other.

Chapter 5: Authenticity, Clarity, and Empathy

1. See, for example, Laura Starecheski, "Take the ACE Quiz—and Learn What It Does and Doesn't Mean," NPR, March 2, 2015, www.npr.org/sections/health-shots/2015/03/02/387007941/take -the-ace-quiz-and-learn-what-it-does-and-doesnt-mean. There are many helpful resources online. The Centers for Disease

Control's website is a good place to learn more about ACEs; visit www.cdc.gov/violenceprevention/childabuseandneglect/acestudy/index.html.

2. See Center for Substance Abuse Treatment, *Trauma-Informed Care in Behavioral Health Services* (Rockville, MD: Substance Abuse and Mental Health Services Administration, 2014), chapter 3, www.ncbi.nlm.nih.gov/books/NBK207191: "Avoidance often coincides with anxiety and the promotion of anxiety symptoms. Individuals begin to avoid people, places, or situations to alleviate unpleasant emotions, memories, or circumstances. Initially, the avoidance works, but over time, anxiety increases and the perception that the situation is unbearable or dangerous increases as well, leading to a greater need to avoid. Avoidance can be adaptive, but it is also a behavioral pattern that reinforces perceived danger without testing its validity, and it typically leads to greater problems across major life areas (e.g., avoiding emotionally oriented conversations in an intimate relationship). For many individuals who have traumatic stress reactions, avoidance is commonplace. A person may drive 5 miles longer to avoid the road where he or she had an accident. Another individual may avoid crowded places in fear of an assault or to circumvent strong emotional memories about an earlier assault that took place in a crowded area. Avoidance can come in many forms. When people can't tolerate strong affects associated with traumatic memories, they avoid, project, deny, or distort their trauma-related emotional and cognitive experiences. A key ingredient in trauma recovery is learning to manage triggers, memories, and emotions without avoidance—in essence, becoming desensitized to traumatic memories and associated symptoms."

3. Proverbs 22:6 ESV.

4. See Numbers 20:6–12.

5. Exodus 2:12.

6. See Deuteronomy 32:48–52.

7. Read the whole story in Acts 9:1–19.

8. Romans 1:1.
9. Daniel H. Pink, *A Whole New Mind: Why Right-Brainers Will Rule the Future* (New York: Riverhead, 2005), 159.
10. Romans 12:15.
11. 1 Peter 3:8 NIV and ESV.
12. Paul received a revelation in Acts 16:6–10 to go to Macedonia and meet the needs of the people there.

Chapter 6: You First: Defining Servant Leadership

1. Proverbs 15:1.

Chapter 7: God + Do = Successful Life

1. James 2:14–26 ESV.
2. James 1:22–25 NKJV.
3. Read the story of the crossing of the Red Sea in Exodus 13:17–14:31.

Chapter 8: "Happy Wife, Happy Life"

1. Read Genesis 2:18 in the King James Version. This is where the term originates.
2. See Ephesians 5:21.

Chapter 9: Create Safe Spaces

1. Read the whole story of Cain and Abel in Genesis 4:1–16.
2. David K. Li, "Hate Crimes in America Spiked 17 Percent Last Year, FBI Says," NBC News, November 13, 2018, www.nbcnews.com/news/us-news/hate-crimes-america-spiked-17-percent-last-year-fbi-says-n935711.
3. "FBI Releases 2017 Hate Crime Statistics," FBI, November 13, 2018, www.fbi.gov/news/pressrel/press-releases/fbi-releases-2017-hate-crime-statistics.
4. Tom Huddleston Jr., "Jessica Chastain and Octavia Spencer Joined Forces to Get Equal Pay," *Fortune*, January 25, 2018, http://fortune.com/2018/01/25/jessica-chastain-octavia-spencer-equal-pay.
5. Cited in Erin Donaghue, "New FBI Data Shows Rise in Anti-Semitic Hate Crimes," CBS News, November 13, 2018, www.cbs

news.com/news/fbi-hate-crimes-up-new-data-shows-rise-in
-anti-semitic-hate-crimes.

6. Cited in Allison Garcia, "FBI: Wisconsin Religious Hate Crimes
More Than Doubled in 2017," Channel 3000, November 13, 2018,
www.channel3000.com/news/fbi-wisconsin-religious-hate
-crimes-more-than-doubled-in-2017/862109714.

7. See "LGBTQ," National Alliance on Mental Illness, www.nami
.org/Find-Support/LGBTQ.

Chapter 10: Change vs. Healing: Hitting the Reset Button

1. 1 Corinthians 3:1–7.

Chapter 11: "That Hit the Spot"

1. Check out Deuteronomy 31:6; Hebrews 13:5.
2. Read 1 Peter 1:3–9 for more information about the inheritance
we receive from God.
3. Mark 12:28–33, emphasis added.